Alice
IN THE COUNTRY OF
Diamonds

BET
ON MY
HEART

STORY
Sana Shirakawa

CONCEPT
QuinRose

ILLUSTRATIONS
Nana Fumitsuki

SEVEN SEAS ENTERTAINMENT PRESENTS

Alice IN THE COUNTRY OF Diamonds

BET ON MY HEART

story by **SANA SHIRAKAWA** / color art by **QUINROSE** / B&W Illustrations by **NANA FUMITSUKI**

TRANSLATION
William Flanagan

ADAPTATION
Lianne Sentar

COPY EDITOR
Shanti Whitesides
Lee Otter

SERIES LOGO
Courtney Williams

MANGA LETTERING
Roland Amago
Bambi Eloriaga-Amago

NOVEL LAYOUT AND DESIGN
Nicky Lim

MANAGING EDITOR
Adam Arnold

PUBLISHER
Jason DeAngelis

FOLLOW US ONLINE: **www.gomanga.com**

READING DIRECTIONS

The manga prelude and epilogue sections that bookend this light novel read from right to left, Japanese style. If this is your first time reading manga, you start reading from the top right panel on each page and take it from there. If you get lost, just follow the numbered diagram here. Enjoy!!

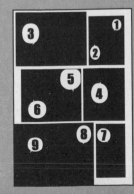

♦♦♦ Cast of Characters ♦♦♦

Alice Liddell

A girl with a few complexes, but who is otherwise normal. After the White Rabbit led her to Wonderland, she decided to stay. She had been gradually adapting to life in Heart Castle, until...

♦ Black Rabbit ♦

Sidney Black

The Black Rabbit who hates Alice. He's a nervous type and always seems annoyed. He hates the color white (and wants to paint everything black)--which obviously puts him at odds with the Queen of Diamonds, who loves white, but he remains a loyal vassal. He develops white hairs from stress, which only serve to increase his stress levels.

♦ Queen of Diamonds ♦

Crysta Snowpigeon

The Queen of Diamonds. Her name and appearance are like a white flag--a symbol of peace--but she's *far* from peaceful. Anything she likes, she freezes and adds to her collection; and right now what she most wants to freeze are Alice and Nightmare. She appears as either a child or an adult.

Joker

A conductor Alice meets while on a steam train. She thinks she knows him, but can't remember. She mustn't remember.

Tweedle Dee and Tweedle Dum

Gatekeepers of Hatter Mansion. Carefree twins who are always coldly calculating. They call themselves the Bloody Twins. Nobody knows which is the elder, and they tend to change their positions regularly. In the Country of Diamonds, they're always in adult form, but their attitudes haven't changed at all. They have an innocent side, but for the most part, they're guided by the devils on their shoulders.

♦ March Hare ♦

Elliot March

The second in command of the Hatter Family. He's very short-tempered, and barely thinks before firing his gun. He's Blood's loyal, adoring dog (rabbit), but he also enrages his boss--which leads to Blood beating Elliot mercilessly with his cane. This Elliot loves carrot-based cooking as much as his counterpart. Some things will never change.

♦ Mad Hatter ♦

Blood Dupre

The boss of the Hatter Family. He's the leader of a Mafia organization, and even more dangerous than his violent underlings. In the Country of Diamonds, the Hatter Family is still maturing, and thus, so is Blood. It seems like he doesn't have as much time for reflection as the earlier versions of Blood.

Nightmare Gottschalk

The Stationmaster of the very dangerous Station, where train accidents are a common occurrence. He's different from the Nightmare Alice knows and takes on a much younger form. He's a sickly dream demon who frequently coughs up blood, but he hates hospitals and needles. He can read minds and has the power to enter people's dreams. He and the old Nightmare seem to be basically the same person, but one could also say they're completely different.

♦ Cheshire Cat ♦

Boris Airay

A Cheshire Cat with a knowing smile. He understood Alice's position as a confused Outsider, so he approached her in a friendly manner. In the Country of Diamonds, Boris lives in the Station. He fixes trains and takes care of the sickly Stationmaster.

♦ White Rabbit ♦

Peter White

The Prime Minister of Heart Castle, despite having rabbit ears. He's the guide who led (dragged) Alice into Wonderland. He loves her and hates everything else. He appears white to her and pitch black to anybody else. His most striking features are his cold-bloodedness and cruelty. Only his beloved Alice can drive him to become a better man (rabbit).

♦ Lizard ♦

Gray Ringmarc

This is a different Gray from the one Alice used to know. He's gone back to his days as an assassin and is gunning for Nightmare. But since Nightmare always looks so ill and timid, Gray never finished the job...and at times, he's even brought Nightmare to the hospital and looked after him. He's much the same as the Gray from before, but one could also say they're completely different.

♦ Clockmaker ♦

Julius Monrey

The Clockmaker, who also goes by the "Undertaker." His job is to fix clocks. He's a cynical mechanics nerd who only steps outside for work. He's ridiculously pessimistic, so he has trust issues. In the Country of Diamonds, he looks after the younger form of Ace.

♦ Gravekeeper ♦

Jericho Bermuda

The Dodo. His role is to run both the graveyard and the art museum. He's also a Mafia boss who stands in opposition to the Hatter Family, so he's a very busy man. The people around him say that he's already dead, but what does that mean?

Ace

This is a different Ace from the one Alice knows from Hearts and Clover. Terrible a directions, he has a tendenc to leave on a trip and never come back. He isn't the sam as the Knight of Hearts, and although he usually appears in young form, he also appears in adult form...?

~Prologue~
Art by Nana Fumitsuki

8

WHAT JUST...?

HEY!

YOU SUCK, YA DUMB BUNNY!

YA MISSED HER. YOU BEEN SKIPPIN' TARGET PRACTICE?

LOOK, SHE'S STILL ALIVE!

SLUMP

....

WHO THE HELL ARE YOU?

DID ELLIOT JUST SHOOT AT ME?!

BLAM

--HERE?

ACT 1

Familiar Friends in an Unfamiliar Country

Alice had no idea what was going on.

Maybe it was just that those treacherous, prankster twins had decided to take adult form and were playing around with their axes. Or were just messing around in general.

But the situation was *shocking*. Had someone told her it was a particularly perverse nightmare, she would've believed it.

"Listen, Alice!" Elliot would always rave. *"There's a new shop that opened a little while back. And the Carrot Mont Blanc there kicks ass!"* His eyes would sparkle, belying his position as the rough, second-in-command boss of the Mob. The *bounce bounce*

of his ears would punctuate his delight.

Alice couldn't count the number of times she'd seen him like that. The only time he'd ever threatened her with a gun was when they'd first met. When they didn't know each other yet.

Yet here she stood, her breath caught in her throat, the sun glinting off the dull metal pointing in her direction. The adult twins stood behind him, their axes ready in their clenched fists.

She made a strangled croak.

Elliot didn't flinch. "Bye," he grunted as he flexed his finger over the trigger.

"What's all this racket? That last job was aggravating *enough,* thank you."

Elliot stopped at the familiar voice from behind Alice. He lowered his gun and stared past her.

Dee brightened. "Boss, you're back! That was quick."

"Welcome home, Boss!" Dum chirped.

Alice sank to the ground, her mind racing. She twisted her head around.

One look at the man walking through the gate made her think her nightmare might be over.

Faceless mobsters started pouring from the mansion, rushing to greet their returning boss. As they spilled out into the open, they lifted their voices in a chant.

"Welcome back, Boss!"

"Right," the man replied, only sparing a quick glance at his people. Then his utterly bored eyes met Alice's.

His clothing was strange: a tailored suit that looked like a cross between formal wear and an equestrian uniform. But there couldn't be *two* men in Wonderland with roses and a numbered card sticking out of his top hat. He ignored the loyal mobsters who crowded around the area, his attention locked on Alice.

She swallowed. "Blood…"

He didn't reply.

Why wouldn't he…?

"Who are you?"

Alice went rigid. "Huh?!"

His stare wasn't the flirtatious gaze she was used to. That rude, searching look from those blue-green eyes…

Her memory pulled her back to the Country of Hearts—when she'd first met him. Blood's gaze had been exactly like this.

The look of someone who doesn't know me.

It was definitely Blood before her, tapping his cane against the ground as he sidled closer. But he kept a healthy distance from her; his appraising eyes were dark with suspicion.

And that suspicion *wasn't* familiar. Blood had *never* been suspicious of Alice in the past—he'd never had any reason to doubt her.

"What are you saying?" As Alice tried to stand up, she pushed a steadying hand against the ground. "I'm—whoa!"

Every mobster in the area pulled out a gun and aimed at her. Her brow creasing, she slowly lifted her hands into the air.

"This isn't funny, Blood! Why are you doing this?!"

He hummed. "I couldn't tell at first glance, but now that I look closer, you're an Outsider. You seem like someone who would only bore me, and yet I drew to a stand at the sight of you, didn't I? Hm."

"Drew to a stand?" Alice furrowed her brow at the unfamiliar phrase. She had no idea what was going on, but at least *this* was familiar—only Blood used such vague phrases.

"An Outsider who isn't used to the world yet, I guess. It's not unheard of…but you're a strange girl. It's death to come here. Ignorance is no excuse, even for an Outsider."

"……"

She waited for him to expand on that, but he said nothing more. Remembering how shaky her legs were, Alice stayed huddled on the ground and held her breath.

"…Have you forgotten me?"

If he had, that would explain the attitude of the people in Hatter Mansion. But the answer to her question didn't come from Blood—it came from Elliot.

"Don't be stupid. Blood's smarter than anyone— he hasn't forgotten anything in his life!"

Alice unconsciously cringed at the force in Elliot's voice. She'd been thrown around this world plenty of times, and she was always facing guns and knives pointed at her…but she wasn't used to the *hatred*. And considering who was throwing it at her now…

Blood seemed to notice her fear, but he only looked curious. He made no move to restrain Elliot, which confused Alice even more.

Even assuming that Blood *had* forgotten her, the Blood she knew would never act like this. He'd play coy and tread lightly—like the way he'd acted when she first met him in the Country of Hearts. He wouldn't be so…defensive.

"Outsiders are rare around here. And even if I don't know you, you seem to know me…which can't be a coincidence." Blood released a breath through his nose. "Fine. Join me for some tea, young lady. I make a rule of inviting people to my tea parties."

He was clearly *pretending* not to care. She could tell he was trying to hide how cautious he was being. Blood was the type of guy to act casual so he could lure an unsuspecting enemy into a trap.

Elliot sucked his teeth. "The hell with this! It was bad enough having the Gravekeeper's men screwing things up. I'd rather just kill you," he added as he raised his gun again.

"K-kill me?"

Alice glanced around at the twins and the other Hatter mobsters in a plea for help, but they didn't seem bothered by Elliot's attitude. If anything, they glared at *her,* as if half expecting her to attack them.

It was all so *wrong*. This wasn't a nightmare—it was worse.

Alice knew how short-tempered Elliot could be—and he seemed worse than usual. If anyone was going to stop him… Her gaze came full circle and landed back on Blood.

Blue-green eyes glittered at her from under that hat brim. He didn't look *completely* indifferent, but if he felt an inkling of sympathy, he didn't act on it. Those eyes said he had no desire to protect her.

She clenched her clammy hands into tight fists.

"Blood!" she pleaded.

"Stop calling the boss by his first name like he's some kinda *friend!*"

Blood cocked an eyebrow at Alice's cry and opened his mouth—but before he could say anything, Elliot advanced on Alice and shoved the muzzle of the gun against her forehead.

"Ah…!"

"I won't miss *this* time, girlie."

Alice couldn't take the pressure of the metal grinding into her skull. She closed her eyes.

Maybe she'd wake up after the gunshot, back in her familiar bed in Heart Castle. A part of her hoped desperately for that. But the chill of the muzzle and the murder in Elliot's voice were too real for a dream.

BLAM

"!"

Her body flinched back—but she felt no impact or pain. She timidly cracked her eyes open as the gunshot's echo faded in the air.

She had no time to be surprised at the rising smell of gunpowder from *somewhere else*.

"Did someone just shoot at us?!" a mobster shouted.

"I'll call for backup!" someone yelled back.

The atmosphere around Alice abruptly changed as the mobsters aimed their guns past her and barked orders. She looked down; a scar charred the ground where a bullet had buried itself. And as she followed the collective gaze of the Hatter Mafia, she finally saw the shadow of a man in the adjacent woods, holding what looked like a lit explosive.

Before he could throw it, fire erupted from the end of Elliot's gun.

"It ain't that easy!"

"Hrgh!" The shadow collapsed with a moan. An instant later, an explosion shook the trees and released a rush of air that reeked of gunpowder.

Elliot jauntily twirled, his brown ears poking up at the sky, then practically scampered toward an exit from the mansion grounds.

"Was that supposed to be an attack?!" he mocked. "The Gravekeeper's punks think we're idiots, huh?! C'mon, boys—you're all with me!"

"Yes, sir."

The Mafia men sounded less than enthusiastic, but they followed Elliot without question—except for the axe-bearing twins standing guard at the door. They simply scowled at each other.

"Hey!" Dee shouted back. "We're not goin'"—

we're doin' our job at the gate. An' we're not your men, bunny boy!"

"Yeah!" Dum agreed. "Runnin' into gun fights is *your* job, bunny barf! I'd never stick my neck out like that without gettin' paid more!"

"Shut up!" Elliot snarled, shooting his gun for emphasis. He was clearly in battle mode. "If you've got time to complain, you've got time to kill something. Move your asses!"

But despite the urgency, Dee and Dum wouldn't even look at him. They shrugged at each other and leaned against the gate.

"Gatekeepers," Blood called, his low voice booming as loud as the gunfire. "Go with Elliot— that's an order. Killing people *before* they break through the gate is part of your job."

Alice had a funny feeling about the new, metallic noises mixed in with the clamor of battle. She turned; sure enough, the click of turning chambers came from Blood's hands. His cane from a moment before had changed.

Now he held a silver pistol.

"What?" Alice squeaked, the word barely leaking

out of her mouth. The question was drowned out by the twins groaning.

"Crap… If it's the boss's orders, we gotta do it, huh? I wanted to clean up that stupid rabbit's mess an' steal the glory."

"Yeah. But remember us bein' so good when you're givin' out bonuses, Boss!"

The twins took off at a light run, grumbling more complaints and demands. Blood didn't deign to reply.

Although Alice felt a squeeze of nostalgia at the sound of their banter, she never took her eyes away from Blood's weapon.

"Is that…new?" she asked, not sure if he could hear her.

The boss of the Hatter Family Alice knew owned a weapon, sure—but it wasn't a pistol. She was used to his rose-covered *machine gun* spitting out a deadly stream of bullets, mowing down anything in his path. This new gun was smaller, sleeker… although the rose design was just as pretentious.

Blood's blue-green eyes snapped to her.

The chill of that gaze dropped her stomach, even

as he flicked it back to wherever he was shooting. He tilted his head at a few remaining servants.

"Take the girl into custody," he ordered. "But don't kill her. Yet."

Panic welled up in Alice again as she scrambled to her feet. Two gun-toting maids popped up on either side of her.

"Yes, sir~!" they chirped.

And with that, Blood turned away and walked out. Alice stared at his retreating back as the maids gripped her arms.

"Now, if you'll come this way~."

"The boss won't let us kill you, but please don't resist~."

Alice swallowed. "I-I know," she murmured weakly. "I'll come quietly."

If Blood's order was the only thing keeping her alive, she knew better than to run. She thanked God the maids wouldn't *casually* murder her, at least.

She let the maids guide her to a wall by the gate. But she had to ask, so she carefully cleared her throat.

"Um, listen. About Blood's...I mean, your boss's weapon. When did he switch from a machine gun?"

She remembered him saying it was "a pain" to switch to a new weapon, so something must have changed…

The two maids tilted their heads in unison at Alice's question. They exchanged startled looks.

"Machine gun~? Did Boss ever use one of those~?"

"I don't know what you're talking about~. The boss has always used a pistol~."

Alice blinked. "Always? That *pistol?*"

Alice expected more of a reaction if they were lying, but the woman nodded breezily.

"Of course~. I remember him saying that he wished it had a little more firepower, but…~"

"Yeah~. But then he decided to keep the pistol and see how things went~."

Alice gripped her temples in confusion. "That can't be right," she insisted. "He—aah!"

A dull *boom* shook the gate that hid them. *Was that a bomb?!* Alice thought frantically as the two maids drew their guns.

Still keeping a watchful eye on Alice, the maids took up positions where they could shoot at the enemy outside the mansion. As Alice clapped her

hands over her ears at the splitting *blam* of their guns, she realized something: at the Hatter Mansion she remembered, nobody was asked to keep their eyes on two targets at once. Blood never gave his Faceless that much responsibility.

It was almost like…the mansion had turned more hardcore. Or Blood was more desperate.

Alice could almost write off the maids' hostility, since she didn't know these particular Faceless; the mansion often changed out servants or gunmen to fight attackers or participate in turf wars. But if Blood, Elliot, *and* the twins acted like they didn't know her, and the attitudes of the entire mansion seemed different…

She kept thinking about that silver pistol. How Blood had "never" carried a machine gun, even if he was interested in it for the future.

She knew, from painful experience, that common sense didn't always work in Wonderland. If some insane truth was staring her in the face, then she *had* to accept it.

Alice gasped, the smoke and stink of iron twining around her body.

"Is this place…the way it was before I *came…?*"

Her tiny voice melted beneath explosions and gunfire. It was so weak, she hardly recognized it as her own.

She didn't want to believe it, but the theory fit. It even explained the battle currently raging so close to the mansion—the first time Alice had met Blood in the Country of Hearts, the Hatters had already claimed this territory, and everyone knew to fear it. Hardly anyone even *visited.*

Alice knew the rumors: if you arrived when the Bloody Twins were at work, you'd be cold cuts in no time. Even if you lucked out and they weren't around, you'd still become a victim of torture for the mobsters who lived inside the mansion. The threatening stories were common knowledge in the territory, which was probably why Alice had never even *heard* of the Hatters having to defend against a frontal assault.

But if this was the past…a world where the Hatters were still building up a reputation and position in the world…

One of the maids made a face at her. "Why do

you keep mumbling to yourself~?" she asked as she fired beyond the gate. "It's dangerous here, you know~!"

"Huh…? Ah!"

A bullet grazed the gate with a high-pitched screech. Ripped out of her thoughts, Alice ducked into a crouch. She'd become used to guns in her time in Wonderland, but that didn't mean she had a death wish.

"They don't give up easily, do they~?"

"Over there~. Here they come~!"

The maids didn't sound nervous as they returned fire, but that didn't make Alice feel better. She scrambled back to her feet and peeked around the gate.

Outside—right around where Elliot had attacked a shadowy bomber—she could see a branch shaking. She hoped the surrounding gunfire and explosions had caused it.

Her stomach tightened as a man jumped out of the shadows of the tree. He raised a gun.

Sweat trickled down Alice's back. "Over there!" she whispered at the maids.

"Could you please be quiet~? We're a little busy here~!"

Alice tried to warn the maids again, but they were too busy shooting. The muzzle of the man's gun trained itself on one of the maids.

Alice didn't stop to think. She tackled the maid to the ground.

"Get down!"

"Whoa~!"

The bullet exploded into the wall above them, sending bits of stone to sprinkle into Alice's hair. The maid twisted up on her knees and returned fire.

The gunman by the tree crumpled to the ground.

Alice breathed a sigh of relief. As the maid pushed herself up to her feet, her gaze briefly met Alice's.

A hint of gratitude flashed on that indistinct face. "Thank you~," the maid breathed.

"I'm just glad you're okay."

The maid resumed shooting by her partner's side as if nothing had happened. Alice got back to her feet and took a small breath.

She had no idea who the Hatter Family was even

fighting. Maybe this was a dispute between mob families, or part of some turf war...or maybe it was just the result of some "rules" Alice couldn't possibly comprehend.

She only knew one thing for certain now: this place was different from the Wonderland she knew. She wiped sweat from the back of her neck as bangs and explosions rang in her ears.

Then, unexpectedly, the sound of gunfire melted away into a flurry of retreating footsteps. Alice blinked as the two maids lowered their weapons.

"I think they're done~. What a pain~!"

"No kidding~! I'm beat~!"

The maids sighed as their eyes met, their guns smoothly flowing from a lowered position to Alice again. Alice stared at the trained muzzles, then raised her hands in submission.

"I know," she said quickly. "I'm not running away."

"She catches on fast, huh~? I still don't know what you were thinking when you covered me with your body~."

Alice let out a breath. "Your boss ordered you to

stand guard over me, right? So is it worth it for me to fight that?"

Alice knew the Role-Holder leader of each territory had absolute authority, especially when it came to Hatter Mansion and its tight-knit mob family. In the Countries of Hearts and Clover, Blood could only accept her as a visitor caught between warring factions *because* he stood at the top of his organization. But now, if Alice's relationship with him didn't exist anymore, all she could do was give up quietly.

"You're a smart prisoner—you should stay that way~. That'll help us out~!"

"Because if you run, even though the boss ordered us not to shoot, we'd still have to kill you~."

"Yeah, right."

Alice couldn't figure out whether they didn't want to shoot her because of the mess it would cause, or because they didn't want to disobey orders. But before she could decide, she heard the sound of approaching footsteps outside the gate—and smelled a drifting stink of iron.

The Mad Hatter—followed by his lieutenants

and Faceless mobsters—walked in, scowling in the aftermath of the battle. Fresh blood was splattered all over the place.

"Ugh," Dee grumbled. "That was kinda sticky. I did a lotta cuttin', but I never thought there'd be so many. I'm pooped!"

"We oughta get hazard pay, Boss!" Dum chimed in.

"Hn," Blood grunted. "Maybe."

Elliot whipped to the twins, his eyes blazing. "You little maggots! We told you it was part of the job—no way are you getting *bonuses* out of it!"

One of the maids guarding Alice took a step toward Blood, her gun still trained on Alice's forehead.

"Boss~... There's something we'd like to talk to you about~."

"...Right now?"

Blood looked like he wanted nothing less, but the maid still started her report. She spoke in a low enough voice that Alice couldn't overhear.

"......"

Alice wondered what the maid was saying. With a restless heart, she stared at Blood...until he turned those blue-green eyes back to her.

They were still cold as ice. She remembered a time when he'd turned that look on her before, but the recollection just made her feel even further removed from the man. He finally stepped toward her, his mouth twisting slightly.

"You protected one of my people, young lady. That was a pretty reckless thing to do... Perhaps you thought you could weasel into my organization that way." He sneered.

Alice couldn't say she'd *never* acted out of self-interest, but this time, she'd had no ulterior motive. She'd simply saved the maid instinctively.

"I just...don't like seeing people *die* in front of me," she argued. "I wasn't trying to win any favors."

"Oh?" Blood seemed mildly interested in that answer. His eyes narrowed beneath his hat brim.

He **is** *like the first time I met him.*

He'd always been so fascinated by unusual things that he couldn't hurt them, even if he knew they were dangerous. It was a bad habit of his. But before Blood could reply, Elliot cut across him.

"Ugh. Are *you* still here?" The March Hare still

hadn't bothered to wipe the blood off his cheeks. He casually lifted his gun.

A shiver ran down Alice's spine. With no apparent hesitation, Elliot put his finger on the trigger.

"Just die, will ya? Pain in the—"

"Wh—NO!"

Alice squeezed her eyes shut as the gunshot cracked. A heavy *thud* sounded at the same moment.

"Nngh…hggh!"

Miraculously, the groans didn't roll up from her own throat. They came from *Elliot.*

Alice opened her eyes and gave a short yelp. Elliot was down on his knees, Blood's foot grinding into the small of his back.

"Who told you to shoot her, Elliot?" Blood murmured, glaring down at his minion in contempt.

"B-but Blood…!"

"We were having a conversation. *Never* interrupt your boss."

"But when she said 'Blood,' she—urg!"

Maybe Blood just wanted to stop the argument; he dug his heel into Elliot's side. He kicked the obviously hurt man again, then whacked Elliot on the head with his cane. Blood flashed a sneer.

"*I'm* the one who decides what happens to the girl. Raise your gun to her again and I'll shoot *you.*"

"S-sorry, Boss…"

"Clearly I need to pound that into your body or it doesn't stick."

"I won't get in your way anymore, I promise!"

"You'd better not."

Alice watched the beating, dumbfounded, but the rest of the Hatter Faceless all averted their faded eyes. None of them complained about their boss's high-handed savagery. Elliot didn't even *resist.*

"……"

Alice felt a sense of déjà vu. She remembered a time not long after the White Rabbit had dragged her to Wonderland—when this kind of cruelty was common within the walls of Hatter Mansion. As time had gone on, she'd witnessed fewer and fewer of those scenes, but they'd probably never stopped completely. Maybe the Hatters had just *hidden* them from her to be polite.

Now, clearly, they didn't feel the need.

The twins suddenly stepped up from behind

Blood, absently twisting their hands over their axe handles. "Hey," Dee interrupted. "If the bunny's punished now, Boss, what *are* we gonna do with her? Ya want *us* to kill her?"

"Eh, I want bonus money if I've gotta do somethin' extra. I hate doin' freebies. We can throw her in the body pile an' add her kill to our bonus cash."

Blood shrugged. "I know the girl looks like trouble, but we can kill her later, if I feel like it. For now, just throw her into one of the cells. At least until we decide how to deal with her."

The maid Alice had saved nodded her head. She lowered her gun and re-gripped Alice's arm.

"As you wish, Boss~. Miss, if you'll come with us~."

Alice recoiled slightly. "If I…have to?"

The maid led her into the compound, and down to the inner depths of the mansion.

Alice had walked the same route countless times in the Country of Hearts and the Country of Clover. The mansion had some different decorations this time around, but it was essentially the same structure as ever.

What country was she in? And *who* was in it? Alice wished she knew who the Hatters had been fighting outside. She had a million questions to ask...

But she knew the Hatters wouldn't answer. Not if they suddenly didn't know her—or couldn't remember her. Whatever the heck was going on.

The maid eventually brought Alice to a basement hallway Alice had never entered before. Alice's anxiety flared up at the dim light and chilly drafts. They walked past a long line of doors until the maid opened one on the end.

"In here, if you'd be so kind~."

"Uh...thanks for the hospitality," Alice muttered awkwardly as she stepped inside.

Her eyes trailed over the stone floors, a bed that could only charitably be called a cot, and a tiny window with iron bars that choked the outdoor light. Like a typical prison, as far as she knew.

As she stared at the cell in a daze, she heard the *clang* and *chak* of the door closing and locking behind her.

They didn't have to lock it, she thought. *They know I'm not gonna run.*

Every employee of the mansion was in the Mob—*nobody* could escape a place filled with gangsters on guard. Even though Alice knew the mansion pretty well, there was no way she could escape without someone noticing her.

With nothing else to do, she sat on the cot attached to the wall. The rock-hard mattress was a good match for the damp air. As she considered sleeping on that thing, her lips unthinkingly curled into a sardonic smile.

"This is actually pretty good treatment for a stranger who just *happened* to appear in a Mafia headquarters." She rolled her eyes up to the ceiling. "At least I'm not being tortured."

Only a few time periods before, the Hatters had insisted she stay as a guest in one of their lavish rooms. And it was more than just her guest room—she'd been invited into the twins' room. Into *Blood's* room.

Each and every room was a top secret within the Mob. But they'd also housed good friends, and so she could easily remember the interiors of all those rooms.

What happened to those friends…?

As she lay down on the cold cot, questions spun through Alice's head. Had there just been another "move"? Did this *count* as "moving"? But she hadn't just gone to a different place—the flow of time seemed to have gone upside down on her.

Alice reached toward the ceiling in the dim light and clenched her hand.

She knew that no matter how much she reached into empty space, nothing would come into her grasp. But she still reached out and closed her hand, over and over.

A queen who constantly lost her temper and ordered beheadings. A strange knight who was always lost. A stalker rabbit who never listened to what *anybody* said. Now she longed for them, but she didn't even know if they existed in this country…

Her vision started to swim. She felt a sudden, heavy drowsiness suck away her strength.

"Huh…?"

Her eyelids fell, as if an unseen hand pressed down on them. Sure, it was nighttime, but she couldn't remember *ever* feeling such an insistent stupor. She couldn't stay awake. Maybe it was physical and mental fatigue after everything she'd gone through.

"......"

She wished that when she awoke, she'd be back in the red castle.

But even as she wished it, some part of her knew it wouldn't come true.

"Please let me know when you're done eating, 'kay~? The boss is calling."

Of all the conversations Alice had had with the maid through the cell door…this was different. She frowned as she accepted the tray sliding through the slot.

"You mean Blood?" Alice asked.

"Yeah~. So eat that up quick, please~. He isn't very good at waiting~."

Alice heard the maid's footsteps quickly tap away. Alice stared at her tray.

She could tell the approximate time period

through the barred window, so she knew it had been about ten periods since she'd been locked up. She figured Blood had his reasons for imprisoning her, but still…this Blood was a little slower to act than the Blood she knew.

Whatever. She was sick of sitting in that dreary cell and twiddling her thumbs. Alice practically inhaled the soup and bread, and by the time she was finished, the maid's footsteps returned.

"Finished eating~? Then come this way~."

A key turned in the door with a *chak.* Alice watched the door finally, *finally* open again.

Even if the maid had heard that Alice was an Outsider, she clearly wasn't taking chances. Another Mafia member stood in the shadows behind her, his gun holstered but ready.

"This way."

The two of them flanked Alice as she carefully stepped into the hallway. As they escorted her out of the prison area, she felt harsh stares from all the Mafia members they passed. But she was just *walking.* How threatening did they think she was?

The Hatter mobsters she knew had always drifted

around with an air of boredom, but these guys were different. It was like…they were restricted, *hardened.*

They passed Blood's bedroom; Alice was instead led to a room way in the back of the living quarters. Alice had a distinct memory of staying in one of these rooms before. Was this the only place Blood would see her now? The maid stopped her in front of a fine set of doors, where two mobsters stood guard.

This was something *else* Alice had never seen— someone standing outside when she visited the boss. After one of the guards rapped on the door, a haughty voice drifted from behind it.

"Enter."

"If you please~." The maid motioned for Alice to go.

Alice sighed. "Excuse me," she murmured.

She passed through the door and into a room that she remembered. It was decorated much like a parlor with two large sofas facing each other. Blood sat in the center of one, and as her eyes met his, the corners of his mouth raised slightly.

An unexpected line of mobsters stood behind him.

"Long time no see, young lady. You look healthy, for a prisoner."

"You're too kind. I should thank you for all your consideration—"

Alice made to casually sit down on the opposite sofa, but she froze at the *clack clack clack* of the men suddenly drawing their guns.

Alice lifted her hands in her defense. Blood snapped his fingers.

The guns returned to their holsters.

Alice was losing patience in this whole mess. She furrowed her brow at Blood.

"You called me here, and you're just sitting there, and you *still* haven't offered a lady a seat. I think that's a little rude."

"It's not very *ladylike* to sit with a Mafia boss without an invitation," he answered thinly. "Now I'll invite you. Have a seat, young lady."

He spread a white-gloved palm and indicated the other sofa. She settled into the seat.

The distance between their couches felt like a thousand miles.

"I'm happy to be out of that dank cell," she said,

"but what do you want from me?"

She tried to choose her words carefully so as not to provoke the mo. rs, but she had a lot of experience with them so she knew she could be direct. The Blood of her experience, as a typical mobster, hated toadying and flattery. She hoped this version of him shared that sentiment.

Sure enough, her words didn't seem to bother him. Quiet the opposite—a wicked smile spread across his face.

"I thought I'd hear what you have to say. The talk we would've had before we were interrupted."

"What talk?"

"I wanted to hear the reason you protected my employee." He impatiently tapped the table.

Blood Dupre, the Mad Hatter, was a territory leader—an extraordinary position among the Role-Holders, someone who attempted to control the game played by everyone living in Wonderland. He tended to be ambiguous, and never relaxed his superior attitude. She liked that flair of his, honestly.

But the actions of *this* Blood were a little easier for Alice to read. Was he acting more obvious on purpose to lure her into a false sense of security?

I doubt it. To him, she was just some unknown Outsider. He didn't need to play tricks.

"Was it that *unthinkable* for me to save your maid?"

"Not unthinkable. Just pointless, as far as I can tell. *You're* not replaceable, so why would you risk yourself for someone worthless like her? It's suspicious."

"*Worthless?* That's a nasty thing to say about your servant!"

The Hatter leaked his breath out in a cold, hissing laugh.

"Have I disappointed you? Maybe, but you can see how baffled I am at your actions. You risked your life for someone else, maybe hoping I'd spare yours in exchange…but life is too cheap in this world for that. It was a stupid thing to do."

"……"

His words were cruel, but Alice gave up on trying to argue with him. She could never successfully talk down the *old* Blood, and he wasn't this…new guy.

"So," she said at last. "You called me here just to tell me my actions were pointless?"

"I'm too busy for that. I want to know what you're *after.*"

"After?"

He slowly nodded his head. "You're an Outsider, but you spoke my name as if we were…close. You knew where this mansion is. Since you seem to know me from somewhere, I need to find out *how much* you know and what you're planning."

He spoke the words with an indifferent air, but she kept catching hints of a threat. She knew being humble was her safest bet.

But Alice decided to talk back.

"Make any assumptions you want," she replied. "I don't think you'd trust anything I could say right now."

"…Oh?"

Blood looked a little surprised, but not angry. A small chuckle escaped his lips.

It was Alice who felt weird at his unexpected reaction. "What?" she asked.

"I never expected anybody to use the word 'trust' when dealing with the Mafia. Or to imply that you want *me* to trust *you*. Should I take it that way?"

"So you're an optimist." She tried to keep her tone light, but her stomach churned.

Of course Alice wanted him to trust her. But because she knew that was impossible at this point, she held back. She felt empty enough without having her hopes dashed.

She looked around. "Does that end the interrogation?" she asked. "If so, I'd really appreciate it if you set me free."

"No, I still have business with you."

"Really? Then could we maybe finish it up quickly?" Alice flashed him an expectant look.

"No matter your goal, the fact is that I still owe you."

"Owe me…? You mean for protecting your maid?"

"Yes. The question is how to make good on the debt."

With a thin smile, Blood peered into Alice's eyes. The intense stare—as if he didn't want to miss anything—was a little different from the stare of the Blood she knew.

But she was still sure he didn't waste time on meaningless words. After all, he was Blood Dupre—

the man who had publically revealed an enemy's secret name, who had a history of fraying people's nerves and making enemies. Whoever the man before her was, she figured the awful parts of Blood's personality weren't going to change that easily.

Before things went from bad to worse, Alice opened her mouth. "So that means you're in my debt, right?"

"I see you finally want something."

Alice ignored the look in Blood's eye that seemed to say, *Not that you'll get it.*

"If you're in my debt, I want you to keep me in the mansion. Is that possible?"

Blood raised an eyebrow. "What does that mean, young lady?"

"It means exactly what I said. I want to stay in Hatter Mansion." She cleared her throat. "I won't go into any area you block off from me, and I'll do my best to stay out of your way. Deal?"

"......"

It looked like Blood wanted to give her an immediate rejection, but then he closed his mouth. He stared at her, searching.

From Alice's point of view, an escape would mean heading into the other territories—and she had no idea what other territories even *existed* here. She wanted to stay with what she knew. Or *used* to know, anyway.

Even if she hadn't saved the maid's life for this purpose, she needed all the help she could get.

Still, her anxieties resurfaced in Blood's unexpectedly long silence. Did she seem *more* suspicious now? Through the pounding of her nervous heart, she blurted, "M-maybe I'm asking too much."

Blood puffed out a short breath.

"You want to *stay?* Even when you seem to know so much about what goes on here?" His thin lips stretched into a smile. "Your mind works in strange ways…even for an Outsider.

"All right—you can stay, if a young lady finds so much appeal in a Mafia stronghold. Are you bored or something?"

Alice felt the blood come back to her face. "I…I *wish* it was just that. But ever since I came to this world, I've never had time to be bored."

It sounded like he was treating her like an exotic pet. *So I'm doomed to that every time I meet him, huh? Ugh.*

"I'm not asking you to keep me here for free. In lieu of rent…well, you can put me to work, if that's enough."

"Work that a little princess like you can do? I'll think about it. But it's a shame."

"What is?"

He tilted his head and lifted the brim of his hat a bit. "I could've had a different kind of fun if you were an enemy operative under cover.

She would *never* be stupid enough to try to slip into Hatter Mansion as a *spy.* "Sorry to disappoint you," she muttered.

He gave a short laugh at her comeback, but it didn't sound relaxed. He lacked that incredible sense of calm from the Countries of Hearts and Clover.

She couldn't "handle" this man. He seemed fiercely private, cold, and intimidating. She could only benefit from his thrill at finding something rare.

"……"

On the other hand, he'd been like that when she'd first met him in Hearts.

She was a rare Outsider. Someone with a real heart who came from a different world. It was the only reason Alice could stay in Hatter Mansion without fearing for her life.

"I'll expect you to show me a good time outside of work hours, too," Blood drawled. "But let's get right to it. If you're going to live in this mansion, you'll follow my one simple rule." He flicked up his index finger. "Never leave the grounds without my permission. If you break that rule and leave the house, we'll hunt you down like a fugitive."

"…You think I could actually run off with your secrets?"

He'd acknowledged that she wasn't an enemy operative, but he was still clinging to his doubts about her? She was a little…wounded, honestly.

He didn't even blink. "I'm allowing an unknown entity to stay close. I think the rule's reasonable. If you're going to argue something this simple, I don't see how you can live here."

"Fine," she said quickly. "I get it, kinda. I consider

myself warned."

Alice still didn't know for sure what kind of man this Blood was, but the back and forth made her feel a little better. He seemed…younger than the Mad Hatter she knew. Like he had the same abilities, but not full control of them yet.

And maybe he lacks confidence.

Just as that thought crossed her mind, the door burst open. Two black shadows flew in.

"Hey, Boss! We got the orders for the next job, but that'd be overtime, an' you said we had a butt-load of vacation time that we could take! Now you're goin' back on that?! We never get to go to the castle an' have fun!"

"Yeah, an' you're sayin' we might not get overtime pay?! *Gah!* Ya gotta motivate your workers, Boss!"

The twins, still in their adult forms, waved their axes around as they complained. It was always a little weird to see them acting like kids in those bodies.

Alice was familiar with that trick—every Role-Holder in Wonderland could apparently advance through time at their own pace, taking on the form of a young or old person at will. More often than not, the Bloody Twins looked like youngish teenagers, not these 20-something adults.

In their underage forms, they were so much trouble that only Blood could tolerate them. As adults, they were even more dangerous, and even *louder.* It was like a storm had blown through.

Blood scowled, his tolerance for them clearly strained. "You two don't know how to shut up, do you? Elliot was supposed to handle this."

As if in response to Blood's words, the shadow of the third man—beast?—came barging into the room.

"You little brats have balls to ignore me and piss off Blood!" Elliot shouted. "I oughta—hrck!"

Blood threw an ashtray at Elliot that knocked the man (beast?) to the floor.

"Shut up, all of you! Didn't I just say that I'm sick of hearing about this?!" Blood took a long breath.

Dee kept going. "Boss—listen, Boss! Isn't there a whole clause about vacation time in our contract? We lose our juice if we don't get time off!"

"Yeah!" Dum added. "We work our butts off an' deserve the extra pay!"

Blood sighed. "The noise never ends…"

The twins spent the next few minutes proving his point, although their clearly annoyed boss wouldn't answer their demands.

Maybe Alice felt a little less tense in the noisy room, because she found herself asking, "Are you two ever going back to being kids?"

After all, they used the "we're just kids" excuse for everything they did, even when no one asked. They'd used that excuse to run wild on *her*.

Alice asked it with a bit of nostalgia in her heart, but the twins just cocked their heads and exchanged glances. When Dee answered, he had an odd tone to his voice.

"What're you talkin' about, lady? Go *back* to bein' kids?"

"Yeah, I just mean—"

Dum laughed. "Man, you're weird! Maybe you think we're somebody else. Nobody in the Hatter territory's gonna hire *kids!*"

"Wait…what?"

Looking at Alice's surprised face, Blood continued where the twins left off.

"You wish they were *younger?* I never thought your tastes would run that way, but... Sorry to disappoint you, but there are no children here. Although you may see some at the upcoming event."

Alice bristled. "Don't talk to me like I'm some kind of pervert, okay? I just mean it feels weird when they... God, how do I put this?"

The first time Alice had ever seen the twins as adults, they'd all been at Assembly in the Country of Clover. After that, whenever she saw them take adult form on a whim, it unnerved her—since she had always thought of them as basically kids.

Elliot had recovered from the ashtray to the face. He twisted his head at Blood as he struggled to his feet.

"Event...? Crap, that reminds me."

Blood sucked his teeth. "Exactly. I know it's a rule, but it's a pain."

"A rule? Do you have to go to an entertainment event again?" Alice asked.

Blood's eyes widened slightly. But he swiftly erased the expression from his face and raised an eyebrow in question.

"How long have you been living in this world?" he asked her. "You call us by name, not by title, and you completely lack respect. And now you know about our *entertainment events?*"

The only "entertainment events" Alice had experienced were the Ball in the Country of Hearts and the Assembly in the Country of Clover. She'd learned all about them by participating.

Was it stupid for me to say that? Blood looked... edgy.

"Um... Yeah, I guess..." She tried to backpedal a little. "I've heard about those events before, but I don't know which ones take place here. Would you please tell me?"

"It's the Survey Meeting," Dee cut in. "But you can make bets, an' there's even a party! Sounds fun, right?"

"You can get rich quick on one bet!" added Dum. "It rocks!"

A Survey Meeting? She didn't know what that meant.

"We'll explain the Survey Meeting some other time," Blood said, as if reading her mind. "All you need to know is that it runs over three separate meet-ups and is a pain in my ass."

"......"

If it didn't end in one meeting, it was closer to the Assembly than the Ball. Alice sucked in a breath.

She needed to mentally prepare before she asked her next question.

The White Rabbit had first brought her to Wonderland, leaving her in the Country of Hearts. The first time she'd "moved," she'd ended up in the Country of Clover.

And then…

She paused.

Wait. Before finally arriving in *this* country, had she wandered into some hallucination, too…?

Shaking off the vague disquiet, she took a breath. "Blood," she asked, her voice trembling slightly. "What *is* this country? What's the name of it?"

She feared the answer. If he told her the name, and it was a place she'd never heard of…she would have to face that reality.

But the Mad Hatter's reply just sounded bored.

"You don't know where you are?" he asked. "This

is the Country of Diamonds—under the rule of the Queen of Diamonds."

"The Country of…Diamonds…?"

It took Alice a long moment to find the strength to nod.

The Country of Diamonds.

Alice rolled around in bed, ruminating over that. She wasn't in a dimly lit cell anymore—which was a plus. She appreciated her new guest suite.

But the new knowledge had set her emotions churning again. She buried her face in her pillow.

"So is that why nobody knows me here?"

She knew that "moving" shifted the landmasses around Wonderland. But nobody had ever lost their *memories* in that process.

Actually, no—the Hatters couldn't have just lost their memories since the last move, since everyone was acting like they were in a time before Peter had even brought Alice to the Country of Hearts. Or they *hadn't* lost their memories, and the Country of Diamonds was a place where Alice had never existed in the first place.

She groaned. "Peter," she grumbled automatically. "Why aren't you here to help me?"

Loneliness welled up in her. She filed internal complaints for the white shadow floating in the back of her mind.

Peter had brought her to Wonderland, by literally dragging her down a hole in her garden. He was *supposed* to be her guide.

Alice still knew nothing about the Country of Diamonds...but she had a hunch that Peter wasn't in it. If he were around, she wouldn't be alone and floundering for answers and recognition.

"......"

When they'd come to Hatter Mansion—no, when they'd entered the Country of Diamonds— Peter had suddenly disappeared in a flurry of rose petals. When she remembered that, an unspeakable emptiness opened inside her.

It wasn't the first time the only person she knew had disappeared in a transition. But losing Peter... she couldn't help but feel that she'd lost something especially precious.

Are Vivaldi and Ace gone, too?

Heart Castle with all its proud red roses. The tea table set there, steam rising from the teacups amidst the huge assortment of sweets.

She couldn't count the number of times the Queen of Hearts had announced a tea party with a bright smile on her face. The White Rabbit would coo Alice's name and guide her through the goodies on the table. The Knight of Hearts would lean over and tease him. She loved that place. It was a precious sight burned into her memory. And even though she knew that common sense didn't work in this world, it was still hard to accept that she could be separated from them that easily.

And even if they *were* in this country, they might be just like the Hatters—people who considered Alice a complete stranger. The thought sent shivers down Alice's spine.

She tried not to think of Peter looking at her with a stranger's eyes.

"...Agh, I can't sleep like this!"

She sat up in bed and shook her head to clear it.

An indigo sky spread out beyond the window.

The maids had warned her that battles raged in every region of the Country of Diamonds, and she'd be wise not to wander, not even inside Hatter Mansion. But that meant she could only sit in her room and wait for the next time period to come.

She frowned. "I wonder if there's something to change my mood... Wait, I know!"

Roses bloomed at Hatter Mansion in both the Country of Hearts and the Country of Clover. She thought a look at them might help her mood... Just imagining it made her heart dance a little.

She threw aside her gloom along with her sheets and hopped off the bed. She needed Blood's permission to leave the premises, but she didn't need that to check something inside the mansion grounds, did she?

She got dressed and headed out. But as she walked through the outdoor grounds, trying to enjoy her little night stroll, she still felt the eyes of mobster servants following her every move.

Supposedly, she was considered a guest now, but the servants clearly didn't accept that. Which probably meant their *boss* didn't accept that.

Alice told herself they just needed time. There was no need to panic yet. But even as she told herself that over and over, she still felt her spirits sink under their suspicious eyes.

She needed that rejuvenating walk among the roses. She needed to feel *better.* But it was that very anticipation that made her crash when she found the garden.

"What the… This can't be right!"

She'd expected a flowering rose nirvana, framing a finely carved tea table and other works of art…a garden to match the one in Heart Castle.

But instead she stared at a dirty spit of land covered in wilting brown plants. A foliage-draped fence only allowed the occasional space for a small flowerbed. Instead of flowers, weeds choked the ground. Alice fell into new misery.

"……"

Maybe it's just this small area? Alice hoped it was an isolated block of rot, but as she walked the grounds, she saw that it wasn't. The entire place was an overgrown, dying mess.

If this was the Hatter garden, and the servants were all tightly wound brutes...Blood probably didn't throw his tea parties at all. This was the Mad Hatter's mansion in the Country of Diamonds?

Alice was honestly shocked.

After a few minutes of walking aimlessly through the ravaged garden, she came to a halt. She thought she saw a long, white shape.

"Huh?" she murmured. "Is that Blood over there?"

As she stared into the darkness, she saw the familiar lines of his back melt into the gloom.

He was a bit too far away to call out to. And more than that, Alice still wasn't sure how to approach the guy.

Curious, Alice started to follow him. Almost immediately, two servants appeared to block her way.

They hadn't drawn their guns, but their smiles were ice cold.

"Sorry, Miss~. No admittance beyond this point."

Alice frowned. "Really?"

"Yes—it's dangerous around here at night~. You should go back to your room~."

Their voices were calm, but Alice could tell that she wasn't going any farther in that direction.

"Okay," she murmured at last. "Good night, then."

"Good night~."

Alice had no real reason to follow Blood, so she was willing to do as she was told. While walking back to her assigned room, she glanced up at the sky.

The half moon loomed like a lord in command of a sky of glittering stars. The moon was the only thing that stayed consistent between the countries of Wonderland, even as its phases forced it through an unending, shifting cycle.

She breathed a heavy sigh at the irony.

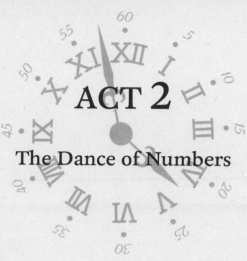

ACT 2

The Dance of Numbers

The books lay stacked up in a mountain under the dim ceiling lights. Alice took a book from the pile and read the title. Her eyebrows drew together.

"*The Finer Points of Converting Heavy Firearms,*" she recited. "What's this doing here? These shelves aren't supposed to have anything to do with weapons."

"Oh, dear. Did one get mixed in~?"

Alice grabbed another book. "Yeah. And this one's *When to Use the Knife, When to Use the Dagger.* This shelf isn't organized at all!"

As Alice pulled out another misplaced book, her shoulders dropped in depression. The book stacks cast dark shadows against the moonlight spilling in from the window.

A maid, her arms overflowing with books, shrugged as she threw a glance at Alice.

"Hardly anyone ever comes into this place looking for books, anyway~. So the people who do just put them wherever they find space~."

"That's no excuse! What's the good of having a reference library if you're just going to treat it like a barn?" Alice grunted. "What a waste of a great library."

She checked another book: *One Hundred Choices for Drugs*. She didn't even flip through that one— she just stacked it on the tower of books about drugs.

As a condition of her staying in Hatter Mansion, Blood had assigned Alice a job: to put the reference library back in order. Or, to be more precise, he had *first* tried making her a mover and then a maid, but after only a short time of each, he'd decided to have her do something else. She'd worked as a maid in Heart Castle, so she knew she'd been handling that one just fine...which meant the Hatters had probably realized that maid's work would give her access to secrets they didn't want her seeing.

Thus giving me the books.

After a few time periods as a librarian, they hadn't shifted her to anything else—which meant this was probably her position now. And she wasn't terrible at it.

She was responsible for re-shelving the returned books in proper order—but before that, she had to find and *clear* those correct spots from the intrusion of other books. Each shelf more or less had a category attached to it, but most of them had books of different sections mixed in. Alice had recruited a maid to help her relocate the interlopers to their proper shelves.

"They call this a reference library," Alice muttered. "But not right now, it isn't."

"It's worth the time to fix it."

"!"

The very words she was thinking materialized out loud, from a low voice behind her.

Alice swallowed the complaint stuck in her throat and turned. Blood walked lazily between the shelves, dragging a finger along the books' spines.

"I...didn't expect to see you here," she murmured.

"I wanted to see how hard a *guest* works." He pulled a book at the edge of his fingertips—something from the section designated for industry technical manuals. "Hm. It's looking more organized already."

Alice watched him silently flip through the book and felt a sense of déjà vu. But not of this dreary reference library...

Just of him. His tilted face in profile as he read a book, time and time again.

In that private room of his, almost a library itself with all its tomes; under the shade in the mansion's garden; and in that hidden sanctuary with all its red roses in bloom. Blood had always loved reading, so they'd spent many a quiet period together, reading in each other's company. Hatter Mansion had been a calm, content place that no one would suspect was a Mafia base. Her memories of that were as precious as those of the tea parties in Heart Castle.

And now, as she stood beside the Blood of the Country of Diamonds, she keenly felt the distance from her past life. As reflections tumbled through her head, Blood abruptly looked up from his book.

"Do you find this work boring?"

Alice blinked. "Huh? No... Not at all. Why would you think that?"

"Because you're just standing there and looking at me."

"Urk. Right, sorry."

The man gave a snort at her meek apology. "If you aren't bored, then I envy you. You won't find a single secret hidden in here—so I thought you might regret the assignment."

"I told you that I'm not after *secrets,*" she reminded him dryly. "Anyway, about this job— this place is a complete mess. How have you been managing it up until now?"

Blood slid his book onto a different stack, possibly answering the question.

Alice sighed. All the reference books in the library seemed useful—even if they were mostly about weapons or drugs or other dangerous things. But out of order, they were useless as *reference*. It was like leaving a treasure trove to rust.

"Don't you have any librarians?" she pressed. "Or

maybe you have plans to hire one…?"

"I doubt there's a mobster in this world who wants to organize a *library*. If I posted a librarian job, we'd get two kinds of applicants: spies, or meek little failures who would be useless in our many gun fights."

"Oh… I guess you're right."

As Alice nodded, a different thought formed in the back of her mind. It would be a risk to hire someone new, especially with all the warring territories and rival mobsters. But there was a problem even before it got to that—Blood and his people had no room in their hearts to even accept *her,* an Outsider. Alice remembered how much mobster fighting she'd seen in the Countries of Hearts and Clover—to say nothing of what she *hadn't* seen, especially since she'd lived in Heart Castle—but still, the residents of Hatter Mansion had never given her the impression that *they* were in fights. They were strong enough to protect her, they just didn't seem… on the offensive.

The Hatters in the Country of Diamonds lived under much stricter rule, apparently. And since

Blood had never seemed like a pushover in Hearts or Clover, maybe that just meant he was…worse at management here. Like he was younger and hadn't gotten the hang of being a leader yet.

She was starting to understand Diamonds Blood a little better.

He flashed her a small, slanted smile. "You're an odd one, to worry about the utility of a mobster's reference library."

"O-odd?"

"Just my honest opinion."

His smile turned nasty as he returned another book to the shelf. She worried he'd only come to make fun of her, but then he moved farther back into the library.

He gazed at the spine of another book, then took it out and studied the cover. He seemed to have forgotten her presence.

"……"

"Uh… What are you looking for?" she asked at last. She *was* supposed to be helping out here.

She thought he'd reject her offer as being none of her business; she was surprised when he obediently opened his mouth to answer.

"I suppose…bring me the records on the residents here. Also, if you have anything that can help me understand the changes in finance, I'd like that even more."

"Sure. I'm kinda surprised you need so much. Can I ask what you'll be using it all for?"

A moment before, he'd been looking at industrial technologies, and after that, information on the forests and rivers in Hatter territory. They didn't seem like anything directly related to the business of running a Mafia organization.

Blood drew a breath. "We already told you— there's a Survey Meeting coming up. I'm trying to prepare."

"Oh. The Survey Meeting…"

She started searching for the books while he continued to explain. She made the occasional noise to let him know she was still listening.

"I don't know how much you've heard about it," he murmured, "but there's a rule in this world that says we have to gather for 'entertainment' at regular intervals. The Queen of Diamonds rules this

country, so she'll be presiding over the meeting…
unfortunately."

Alice headed for a different bookshelf to poke
around for what he needed. It took him out of her
line of sight.

"If it's supposed to be 'entertaining,' what do
you do in it? You're not going to do a survey to see
which lord of which territory is tallest or something,
right?"

"We survey the *power* of each territory," Blood
said coolly.

Alice stopped at that. She peeked through the
shelf; the back of his white suit jacket faced her, his
eyes firmly fixed on the reference book in his hands.

"Power," she repeated slowly. "So, like…the
relative size of each territory?"

Blood didn't turn. "Overall area is *part* of it,
since we try to claim each other's territory. But
nothing is gained through size of territory alone. I
wouldn't call trying to survey something that can't
be surveyed *entertaining*," he added dryly. "The
entertainment comes from taking the size of the
territory as a foundation, and building on it by

converting other types of power into numbers."

"Numbers?"

"Yes. This world *overflows* with numbers. You could say gathering numbers is this world's best entertainment." He let a breath out through his nose. "So the Survey Meeting takes those gathered numbers and compares them."

Alice grunted her confusion. The one thing she *did* understand was this was very different from any friendly gatherings and masquerade parties. She kept scanning the book spines and humming affirmatives as he went on.

"This may be difficult to understand for a prim and proper girl like yourself," he commented. "But to put it simply, it's like a card game you would find in a casino. Each territory leader holds the five forces of his territory in his hand: natural resources, population, military, economics, and technology. Only the leaders can correctly interpret these powers and judge how powerful each individual force is in his territory." He snapped his book shut. "And then he plays one force at a time against the other territories in hopes of dominating."

Alice mulled over that. She could understand parameters like "natural resources" and "technology," but "population" made her knit her eyebrows together.

She knew a lot about the...oddities of this world. She knew the people had clocks in their chests instead of hearts, and that that was how they were recognized by others in Wonderland—as being embodiments of time.

"So...you're saying the leader controls the population, and they can be forced to work in cooperation with you?"

If it were a card game, the population would be nothing more than a hand of cards.

Alice heard a hint of her disgust leak into her voice. She grabbed the last needed book and carried the stack back to Blood. He looked up from his book at just that moment, and their eyes met.

She thought he'd return to reading once she handed him the books, but his arm just curled over the stack while he kept his gaze locked on her.

"Hm..."

"Wh-what?" she blurted. "If you have something to say to me, then don't hold back."

"I just thought you'd be more surprised or tell me you didn't understand. You know this world a bit more than I expected you to. Why don't you tell me where you learned all that, young lady?"

She paused. "Not from you," she finally answered, tapping the books in his hands. "These the ones you needed?"

It wasn't a lie. No one had put any information *specifically* into words. But as she'd interacted with the people of Wonderland, she'd naturally increased her knowledge of how their world worked. Her understanding advanced accordingly.

He finally drew a breath and shrugged.

"The Survey Meeting is just tedious," he said. "Going out in a daytime period is already annoying, and gathering the necessary information makes it worse. It's one giant pain."

He looked exasperated by the whole affair. She nodded her response, then added, "Will you need any other reference books after this?"

"Probably. My main role in the Survey Meeting is to understand my nation's power."

"Okay. Just give me some advance warning next

time and I'll grab the books before you come. It'll save you time."

"……"

Alice just considered this a natural extension of her job (and thus earning her keep), but something twinkled in Blood's eye.

"You're a strange girl. You're willing to take on headaches for a Mafia boss who won't repay the kindness."

"It's not strange. You said I should organize and maintain the reference library. That's my…well, for now, that's my *role*."

She knew that as an Outsider, she was always going to be treated a bit like an exotic zoo animal—but she got the feeling that Blood was treating her that way for his own reasons as well.

"I suppose you're right. You're our best librarian now. Personally, I'm so busy with work that I can't spare a moment—I need to get these pain-in-the-ass projects off my desk as soon as possible."

He nodded at Alice with a hint of amusement, but didn't say anything more. He tightened his grip on the stack of books in his arm and headed for the exit.

Just as he was about to leave, the maid from earlier popped her face in the room. Alice blinked; she hadn't seen the woman leave.

But I didn't hear her while I was talking to Blood. Since she'd been ordered to help Alice, did that mean he'd ordered her to *leave?*

"Is your discussion all finished now~?"

"Ah, yes. Please continue your work here."

"I suppose we have to, no matter how annoying it may be~."

As the two of them spoke, the color of the light streaming through the door changed. The moonlight shifted into the golden light of day.

Alice let out a breath. She beckoned the maid over, ready to battle the clutter beast until the next time period.

The town serving the castle was decorated with a diamond motif, with everything integrating the color yellow. The townspeople milled in one big mass toward a single destination. Flanked by Blood,

Elliot, the twins, and a few other Hatter Faceless, Alice twisted her head around to look at the territory run by the castle.

"Come to think of it," she said aloud, "this is the first place in the Country of Diamonds I've gone to aside from Hatter Mansion."

She wasn't sure if this was typical of the place, but the lively atmosphere showed all the signs of a festival. She overheard the conversation of two men who stepped out of an alleyway.

"Hey, who're you betting on this time? I'm thinking of throwing my money on the Station."

"Y'know, I've been thinking that—wait, those are the Hatter guys! Watch your mouth!"

"Crap!"

The two animated men suddenly shut their mouths and dropped their eyes to the ground. They tried to nonchalantly put some distance between themselves and Alice's group.

Alice tilted her head in curiosity. "Did you hear that?" she asked the others. "Are people *betting* on something?"

The twins—who seemed the most excited to be

out of Hatter Mansion—blinked big eyes at her.

"Ya didn't know, Big Sis? Everybody else joins the Survey Meeting by gamblin' on it. That's why it's like a festival out here."

"Gambling?"

"Yeah. They bet on stuff like the rankin' of each territory. You can win big on a meeting like this."

Alice frowned. "But aren't there only five types of forces? Doesn't that sort of limit the ways to win?" *If there's a strict limit on the cards,* she added silently, *that means the same outcomes happen over and over...*

Dee shrugged. "There's five forces in each territory, but there are three Survey Meetings. An' there's a rule you can only use one force per meeting."

"You keep your strongest force in your hand," Dum added, "an' only bring it out when the time's right an' you can reverse your fortune. An' *make* a fortune!"

"Yeah, but sometimes you don't wanna let anyone see your other forces. It keeps the enemy from knowing what you've got."

"But since there's three Survey Meetings, even if you use all the forces you can, there's two you'll never show." Dum beamed. "Pretty cool, huh?"

Alice mulled over that for a second. "I think I get it. And the strategizing continues between meetings?"

"Yup. You can show a strong hand an' pressure everyone, or make 'em underestimate you by showin' a weak hand."

Clearly, this was yet another way the leaders could perpetuate their fight over territory. Even their muscle-flexing entertainment never exposed all their forces.

But the twins, especially Dum, seemed to have a different reason for the twinkle in their eyes.

"Makin' a fortune," Dum said dreamily. "I like the sound of that!"

Elliot made a face. "These Survey Meetings are annoying as hell," he muttered. "I don't get the attraction. It's just too convoluted."

Alice smiled nervously. "Sounds like it might be."

"Nah," Dee interrupted. "Once it's started, it pretty much runs itself. Like the hands of a clock."

"Hm…"

As they walked through the streets, Alice saw

how much the citizens around them were creeping away. She had never liked crowds, so the little circle of privacy (fear?) around the Hatters was a blessing. Sort of.

They were in a castle's territory, but it wasn't Heart Castle. She didn't know *anyone* in Diamond Castle.

Maybe Elliot noticed her jittery steps, because he snapped, "Hey! Don't wander off—we're not gonna look for you if you get lost. And you know what happens to little girls who wander off, right?"

"I'm staying with the group," Alice retorted. "I'm just…curious about this place, since it's the first time I've been here."

"Not sure I buy that," he said coldly. "And I *still* don't buy that you're a 'guest' of ours. Make one false move and…"

Maybe it was because Blood stood between him and Alice, but Elliot never drew his gun. Alice shuddered—the Elliot of this country had an even worse temper than the Elliot she knew. As she waved her hands to show that she wasn't doing anything, Blood opened his mouth.

"Elliot's right. I see nothing enjoyable in chasing you down."

Without thinking, she turned to glare at Blood. "Listen, you…"

Blood let out a wicked chuckle.

Ugh. He was playing with her like a toy. She wished he'd stop using her to distract himself from the Survey Meeting.

The twins suddenly jumped out in front of Blood, drawing their axes excitedly.

"Hey, hey, Boss! Can we go to the Garden Party? It smells sooooo good!"

"An' we gotta collect info to place our bets right. Play real good this time, Boss! We don't wanna lose!"

"Save it for later," Blood answered evenly. "The bookies at the Garden Party aren't going anywhere."

Elliot growled. "I told you not to bother Blood, you little spit-stains!"

The conversation descended into backtalk again. None of them were willing to give an inch—they all just took a mile. More than a mile.

Their arguing was more confusing than usual, so Alice couldn't find a way to butt in. She winced at the shrieks and stopped walking. The arguing group continued on, granting her a little blissful space.

"Phew." She rubbed the back of her neck. "I guess I'm not in the mood for a loud festival today."

Most of the townspeople were the Faceless—people without roles in Wonderland. Their faces were a little indistinct, admittedly. They bustled around her, festive and animated…even if they were hard to tell apart.

Alice knew getting depressed wouldn't help her. Maybe she hadn't chosen to go to the baffling Country of Diamonds, but she *had* made a decision to stay in Wonderland. She needed to take the craziness in stride.

She clenched her fists. *Cheer up,* she told herself firmly.

Someone grabbed her from behind.

Alice's mouth fell open in surprise, but a hand clapped over it before she could scream. Strong arms pulled her back.

"Mrrf!"

"Shut up!" someone hissed. "We'll let you go when we're done with you."

Adrenaline raced through her limbs, and she struggled in the man's grip. She dragged his hand off her mouth, but new hands and arms suddenly rushed her backwards, dragging her into an alley.

"Wh-who are you people?!" she cried.

Her voice echoed in the alley, but they didn't answer until they'd shoved her far away from the open street, blocking it with their bodies.

They were Faceless men—dressed in black suits. One of them sneered.

"You really don't know who we are? You're pretty slow on the uptake for a Hatter stooge."

Enemies of the Hatters? she wondered, her mind racing. *Do they want to ransom me?* That didn't bode well for her, since the Hatters didn't care much about her in this country.

She shoved the last arm away. "I have no idea who you are," she snapped back. "Don't touch me!"

"Whatever," one of the men hissed. "You know what hand the Hatters are going to play, right? Spill it!"

"What *hand* Blood's going to play…? You mean at the Survey Meeting?"

"Obviously! Maybe he didn't tell you everything, but he must've let some details slip!"

"We know you're close with the Hatter—you live with him!"

"……"

The men wanted secrets for the *Survey Meeting*. Alice was so stunned that she stepped back.

Her shoulders slumped as the strength drained out of her.

"Close" with the Hatters. Is that how people saw her in the Country of Diamonds? *Really?* She had a reputation when she'd spent so long in Blood's *prison?*

The implications of it all made her head hurt. She angrily shook her head.

"I'm not a member of the Hatter Family, okay? I don't know anything."

"Bull. You live in—"

"Yes," she said sourly. "I live in Hatter Mansion. *That's it.*" She didn't add the part about being constantly under watch there.

As she started to think that maybe she'd chosen the wrong place to stay, the men blinked at her.

"You're kidding," one of them murmured.

"According to **our** boss…"

The men exchanged confused glances, and Alice felt the tension of the "kidnapping" drain away. These men didn't seem violent. Heck, they hadn't pulled a gun on her, unlike her hosts at the mansion.

Another voice suddenly echoed in the alley. "According to *me,* what?"

Alice stopped. She didn't recognize the low, gritty voice with a soft edge.

She looked up to see a tall, broad man saunter in behind the Faceless goons. As he neared, she saw the sharp outline of facial features…which meant he had a role. A Role-Holder of some Diamonds territory.

She'd never seen him before in her life.

Glasses rested on a strong nose, but they didn't cover the scars crisscrossed over his face—a stark contrast to his calm expression. He wore a black suit similar to the Faceless, but with a badge on his left lapel.

The Faceless men seemed stunned to see the man in glasses; they scratched their heads in obvious confusion.

"B-Boss…"

"What are you doing here?"

"I could ask *you* the same question. You all disappeared on me, and now I find you roughing up innocent citizens? Watch it. You know trouble's not allowed during the Survey Meeting."

"W-we're sorry."

"We just thought that if you knew what hand the Hatter was holding, you could take him down easier—"

"You shouldn't have done this."

The "boss" sounded like he was scolding a group of children. The Faceless men all bowed their heads in unison.

With a wry smile, the scarred leader turned his attention on Alice.

"I'm sorry for the trouble, miss."

Alice was surprised at the apology. She brushed out her skirt.

"Uh…it's okay? They didn't…hurt me or anything…"

The man stared at her face for a moment. "You're an Outsider?" he murmured. "But you…seem pretty comfortable in this world."

"I wouldn't say I'm *comfortable* with everything, but... Yeah, I'm an Outsider."

She remembered her somewhat hyper reaction to similar words when she'd first arrived in Hearts. But now she just nodded.

The corners of the man's mouth curved up. It softened his rough features.

"Gotcha. Sorry again."

"Why are you sorry agai—whoa!"

The man suddenly pulled her against his body and leapt down the alley, the action so rough that Alice's feet dragged across the concrete. Alice gasped her surprise as bullets exploded the bricks behind where they'd been standing.

The Faceless men scattered. "It's the March Hare!" one of them shouted.

"Don't shoot at our boss, you bastard!"

Elliot bared his teeth from the far end of the alley, smoke swirling from the barrel of his gun. But he ignored the Faceless; his furious eyes were locked on Alice.

"What the *hell* did you tell the Gravekeeper?"

Alice's heartbeat thundered in her ears. "G-Gravekeeper?" she stuttered.

"I knew it!" Elliot snarled. "I *knew* you were in cahoots with that asshole!"

Alice jerked her head at the man who slowly released her. He flicked his ocean blue eyes at her.

He shrugged.

"The Hare's always had an itchy trigger finger." He looked up at Elliot. "It's forbidden to attack members of other territories during the festival."

Elliot cursed. "What do I care about that?! Tell me straight, Gravekeeper—is the girl your spy?"

"Well, no, but I doubt you believe me."

The Gravekeeper. She'd heard that name in the Country of Diamonds. Elliot had called him the enemy…which she believed, considering Elliot had shot at the guy in broad daylight.

The Gravekeeper made no sign of drawing a weapon, but Elliot kept his finger on the trigger. Elliot slowly advanced; Alice stayed stock still, her heart racing.

When the Gravekeeper made a slight move to back off, Elliot's free hand shot out and clamped over Alice's wrist.

"Ow!"

Elliot clearly didn't care about her cry of pain as he roughly dragged her toward him.

"Shut up. I'm taking you back to Blood—*he'll* get you to talk!"

"You're hurting me!" Alice snapped back. "Quit being so rough!" She tried to pry her arm free, but it didn't do her much good. And it only seemed to stoke Elliot's anger.

"I told you to *shut up!*"

Alice winced as he squeezed her harder. "S-stop it!"

"Hey," the Gravekeeper suddenly bellowed. "My men grabbed *her.* You don't have to—"

"You stay outta this!"

The Gravekeeper sucked his teeth. "I don't believe this guy," he murmured in quiet surprise.

But Alice barely heard it; Elliot had stopped dead still in the alley, causing her to stumble right into his back.

Blood stood before him, blocking the way to the street. His blue-green eyes were ice.

"What do you think you're doing, Elliot?"

Elliot straightened. "B-Blood! I finally found her. And like I thought, she—gah!"

Elliot's attempt to shove Alice forward was thwarted by Blood's cane whipping across his face.

"I asked you a *question,* Elliot," Blood said thinly. *"What do you think you're doing?"* He flipped the cane in his hand and swung it, hard, into Elliot's side. Elliot cried out and hunched over.

"I ordered you to bring her back. Did I tell you to hurt her?"

"Nngh…ggh!"

As Blood mercilessly beat his subordinate, Elliot didn't try to run or even defend himself—he just let Blood whack him over and over with the rod. Elliot's weakening grip slid off Alice. She didn't know what to do, so she just stood there, watching in horror.

Even when blood welled up at the corners of Elliot's mouth, Blood didn't stop.

"Answer me, Elliot! Did I tell you to do that?!

"No, you…y-you didn't!"

"Then why don't you *listen to me?*"

Wham! Blood jammed the end of the cane into Elliot's solar plexus. Elliot's tall form finally collapsed to the ground.

"Koff...augh..."

"Why do I have to *constantly* tell you not to go beyond what I order you to do? You know that if I can't keep you in line, everybody will think I can't even housebreak a pet!" Blood rammed the bottom of his boot into the back of Elliot's head. As Elliot curled against the concrete, Blood walked around him, his furious eyes on Alice.

Alice automatically recoiled, bracing herself.

But Blood simply took her hand, turned his back on the Gravekeeper, and walked back toward the street. Shocked into silence, she just ran to keep up with his quick steps. He didn't even spare a glance for the fallen Elliot.

Alice swallowed. She turned to look back, but the Gravekeeper and his men were already leaving, their backs to her as they exited the opposite end of the alley.

It was clear that both he and Blood were pointedly *not* looking at each other. It felt less like an argument and more the evidence of a deep, dangerous rift.

"W-was that the Gravekeeper?" Alice ventured quietly.

"Yes. That's the first time you've seen his face?"

"Um…yeah." Alice took a breath. "What's he the leader of?"

"The Gravekeeper territory, obviously. He runs the graveyard and the art museum."

"Art museum?" Alice repeated in surprise. "That's… not what I would usually lump in with a *graveyard*." Running a place to exhibit beautiful art while at the same time managing a place where people mourned for the dead… She imagined he was an odd leader.

And what counted as a "grave" in Wonderland, anyway? When the people in that world "died," their bodies vanished. All that remained were stopped clocks that had once ticked away in their chests— and Julius was supposed to fix those.

As she wondered about that, she murmured, "He dressed kinda like you, Blood. I thought he was Mafia."

"That's because he is."

"Huh?"

Blood's reply stopped her short. He continued a few steps past her before stopping himself and turning around.

The anger in his eyes had vanished, replaced with an amused gleam. He seemed to enjoy her reaction.

"His name is Jericho Bermuda," Blood explained. "He oversees the graveyard, directs the museum, and yes, he is *also* a Mob boss. I don't know how he looked to you, but he and I are villains of the same stripe." His mouth slanted. "If you think he's going to ensnare you, you'd better be prepared for the consequences."

Alice grimaced. "Thanks for the warning," she muttered.

Footsteps slowly tapped from behind them. Alice glanced back to see Elliot, hunched over slightly, his fists rubbing at the blood that had leaked from his puffy mouth.

Alice knit her eyebrows together at the pained look on his face. She leaned in to whisper to Blood.

"I know this might sound...weird coming from me, since you technically helped me, but...maybe you overdid it with him."

"I have my own ways of doing things," Blood replied coolly. "Don't tell me how to train my dog."

It was clear that he didn't want her opinion—and her being an Outsider probably didn't help. She pursed her lips and gave up.

There was nothing between her and these people that resembled trust or friendship. He was just her landlord now...and nothing more.

The territory leaders were supposed to gather in some waiting room. When Alice asked about the Survey Meeting itself, Blood told her it would take place "close by."

By the time Blood and Elliot brought her to a massive building, the twins had disappeared from their waiting spot. Blood didn't seem surprised.

"I'm sure they'll show up again when they feel like it," he hummed. He gestured to the door. "Ladies first."

Alice paused, then walked through the huge doorway.

The waiting room beyond was already milling with people. Were they all Role-Holders here?

"An Outsider!" a youngish voice called. "That's pretty rare! But still, you don't act like a stranger…"

Alice turned to the young man who bounded to her side. Based on the clarity of his facial features, he had to be a Role-Holder…even though she didn't know him.

Wait. She felt a strange sense of déjà vu as she stared at him. He wore an eye patch over his right eye, his feminine face strangely pale. It was his purple lips that made her think of someone she *did* know.

"What?" she breathed. "You can't be…"

"Hm?" He blinked his one visible gray eye at her. "Do you and I know each other?" He suddenly beamed. "Wait, of course you know *me*. I'm the great and powerful Stationmaster, Nightmare Gottschalk! In the flesh, ha ha ha!"

He puffed out his chest, belying the thinness of his body. But half a moment later, a large shadow descended from behind.

"Big words for someone who always folds right

after starting," a familiar voice grunted. "Don't act stupid, or killing you will seem too easy. If you have time to preen, then you have time to go to the hospital."

Alice's eyes widened at the tall, dark-haired man she knew well. He'd lost his familiar suit and tie, and instead wore a rougher ensemble, including a black coat accented with a purple scarf.

The boy—Nightmare?!—scowled. "Don't you dare be so rude to me, Gray! I don't need the stinking hospi—HRRK!"

Gray narrowed his eyes as the boy hacked out a few watery coughs. "You're proving my point," he said thinly. "Go to the hospital, heal up, and then come back to get slaughtered."

"I-I'm not going to go through that just to get killed! I might as well stay sick! I'm *not* going to the hospital, got it?!"

"You don't care about being killed—you just hate *doctors*. This isn't on me."

It wasn't just Nightmare's boyish form that surprised Alice—it was Gray's attitude toward him. Back in the Tower of Clover, Gray had gallantly protected Nightmare, even going to unwanted lengths to take care of his boss. He'd practically been Nightmare's *mother.*

She'd heard the rumor that once, long ago, Gray had been a hitman gunning to kill Nightmare. Was *this* what he had been like?

As the implications dizzied her, something soft touched her back. She jumped in surprise.

"Eek! Wh-who's that?"

"I was about to ask *you* the same thing."

A young man with fluffy pink cat ears and a striped fur wrapped around his shoulders slid in front of her. He flashed an achingly familiar smile.

"Nice to meet you, Miss Outsider."

Alice's chest tightened. "Boris," she whispered.

He pushed long bangs from one curious golden eye, eliciting a slight *jingle* of his many earrings. "You know me? Did the Stationmaster point me out or something? Man, I hate when people talk about me before I get here."

He seemed depressed for a second, but then he suddenly laughed. The fangs protruding slightly from the corners of his mouth were rather cute, but his most identifying features were the mercurial, ever-changing expressions on his face.

She could see in his eyes that he didn't recognize her—like everyone in Hatter Mansion. Frustration welled up in her chest at the thought that she was at square one with him, too.

*With **everyone**, maybe.*

But there was nothing she could do about it. She smiled at him, and it wasn't entirely forced.

"Nice to…meet you. I'm Alice Liddell. I hope we can be friends."

He saluted her. "Alice. Cool."

Something caught his eye; Nightmare and Gray behind her, apparently. He stepped past her to head for them. Her eyes followed his swishing pink tail.

"I must warn you," lectured another voice. "We have to move forward on the preparations! It's almost time to start…"

"Sidney, you're always bullying me! It isn't right to torture little kids!"

Those voices *weren't* familiar. Alice looked up as a small entourage approached.

They were all wearing black suits, like the

mobsters in Hatter Mansion—but Alice was starting to think there was a rule that all crews coming to the meeting had to wear black suits. One of the figures in the front—a young girl with a clearly defined face, which meant she had a role—had impressive-looking gold trim on her black dress. She flicked yellow-green eyes at a man lurking in her shadow.

"I'm doing my best," she complained. "The least you could do is praise me a little!"

"You're the *host* here, Your Majesty. Please act accordingly. I find it very uncomfortable to have my queen made a laughingstock."

As they neared, Alice saw that he wasn't just a man. He was a…rabbit.

The man had floppy black ears to match his dark hair. His eyes were two different colors—one gray, one red—and a monocle rested delicately over the ruby eye.

The girl suddenly met Alice's startled gaze. She instantly lit up and ran toward Alice.

"An Outsider!" she cooed. "What a treat! And the fact that you're here means that you're doing us the honor of attending our Survey Meeting? As a rule, you'd be ordered to attend an audience at the castle, but I think I'll make an exception in your case. Welcome!"

Alice straightened. "Um, thank you!" she blurted in response.

Based on the girl's words and the fact that the rabbit had called her "Your Majesty," Alice could guess who *this* was. "You must be the...Queen of Diamonds, right? Your Majesty?"

The girl beamed. "Yes, I rule the Country of Diamonds. My name is Crysta Snowpigeon. Welcome, Miss Outsider."

Alice felt put on the spot as she didn't know anything about the girl, so she opted for overly formal. "My name is Alice Liddell. Please accept my apologies for not presenting myself to Your Majesty before this..."

"Please! Don't be so formal." Crysta grinned. "I won't tolerate rudeness from anyone *else* here, but you're an Outsider. You don't know the rules of this world."

"You're so gracious, I don't deserve it."

For whatever reason, the conversation seemed

to irk the rabbit man; his black ears twitched and trembled.

"Your Majesty," he cut in. "We're about to begin. You *must* play your part as host!

"For goodness' sake, Sidney, stop repeating yourself! We just got here." She sighed. "I'll go if I must. Let's chat afterward, Alice."

At the urging of her retainer, the Queen of Diamonds jauntily turned. She strode off, the black rabbit named Sidney scuttling after her.

The Black Rabbit, Alice thought. *The opposite of the White Rabbit, I guess.* He looked nothing like Peter.

"......"

But even so, just for a second, the two converged in Alice's mind. She wiped the overlapping images away.

Thinking of Peter made Alice feel worse. Gloom settled on her shoulders in bitter reality.

She'd met the Black Rabbit's eyes for a second, but he hadn't talked to her directly. She'd sensed cold indifference from him...even a little hostility.

The chorus of voices around her sounded like

other territory leaders and their subordinates talking in bored voices. She heard no room for her to join in, so Alice just let out a breath.

*I really **am** in a country where nobody knows me.*

She almost wished she were as ignorant of them as they were of her. Seeing all those familiar faces was a double-edged sword: she was glad so many of her friends were here, but she was depressed they didn't remember her. She wasn't sure which feeling was stronger.

She didn't have long to ponder it, because Blood practically materialized beside her. "You managed to get close to the queen," he drawled. "Not bad."

"She's only interested because I'm an Outsider," Alice replied. Her voice sounded weak in her ears.

In a country where no one knew her, her position as an Outsider was the only card in her hand. People wanted to *indulge* an Outsider. It was probably the only thing keeping her from getting shot, intentionally or otherwise. At least Blood was sorta her guide now.

She tried to bury her depression. "Did you ever find Dee and Dum?" she asked him.

His eyes narrowed slightly. "Yes, but I left them with Elliot. I can't hear myself think once they start screaming at each other."

Based on the look on Blood's face, Alice decided to change the subject. "I would, um, really like to know more about the territories in the Country of Diamonds," she said carefully. "Who are the other leaders?"

Blood crossed his arms. "There are four territories, including Hatter Mansion—the others are Diamond Castle, the Train Station, and the Gravekeeper's museum and graveyard."

"I guess Diamond Castle is run by those two I just met. Crysta and…Sidney, was it?"

"Right—the Queen of Diamonds and the Black Rabbit. The Station has the Stationmaster, the Lizard, and the Cheshire Cat. But you seem to know them already, so maybe you didn't need the explanation, after all."

She was pretty sure Blood hadn't been nearby when she'd spoken to the others, so maybe he had someone following her?

He's as sharp as ever.

"Okay. Is there anyone else at the graveyard and museum? Besides Jericho, I mean."

"Yes—he has two other Role-Holders in his territory. One is—"

A loud voice squawked through the room, cutting Blood off.

"Julius, you're…strangling me!" a young man cried. "I can't breathe~!"

"I don't like how you're wandering around and *eyeing* everything. Walk in a straight line, Ace!"

Alice sucked in a breath. She whipped around to see a familiar man toss his long hair over his shoulder and drag in a young teenager.

"Wh…"

"Speak of the devil," Blood murmured. "There they are. But it seems like you already know them?"

Alice swallowed. Julius Monrey, the Clockmaker, looked and sounded just like she remembered—but the rambunctious teenager he towered over wasn't the Ace she knew. Was he not the Knight of Hearts anymore? And why was he younger now, like Nightmare?

Julius's blue eyes locked on her and Blood, then

slid past them to the rest of the room. The spark of suspicion in his eyes confirmed what she already guessed: he didn't remember her, either.

The last vestiges of hope died inside her. Now she'd met them all. And not one of them knew her.

"At last," someone called. "I'm sick of waiting. Since everyone is finally here, shall we proceed to the meeting place?"

Alice paused; the words sounded like Crysta's, but her voice was different. She craned her neck to find out who was speaking just as the sound of a loud clap filled the room. Before the reverberations died down, the scene shifted around Alice.

At first Alice thought that the waiting room's walls had just vanished, but then she turned around. She and the other participants stood in a wide, rounded space like a Roman Coliseum, with countless Faceless citizens looking on from the stands.

Alice had *thought* she was used to the casual magic that popped up in Wonderland, but her eyes still widened at the abrupt change. Blood laughed.

"Follow me—our seats are over there. Why do you look so shocked?"

"I just wasn't...expecting to teleport or whatever. Who's the woman who made that announcement?"

"What do you mean? I just told you. Take your seat."

She finally followed his pointing finger; Elliot, the twins, and several other Hatter mobsters sat in a line of nearby chairs. He parted from her side and headed to a chair at the head of the section. His chair—with its fancier upholstery—sat in the front row.

A seat for the leader.

Dee squirmed in his chair. "It's about to start, Brother! Ah, I wanna go to the Garden Party—I hope they set us free quick."

"I'm more worried about our bets, Brother. I wanna double our money!"

Alice lowered herself into a seat next to the twins. She looked out ahead of them, to the middle of the Coliseum, where four giant, hollow, diamond-shaped glass sculptures loomed over the ground. She scanned the faces in the assembled groups.

They went from right to left: the Gravekeeper, Nightmare the Stationmaster, the Black Rabbit, and finally themselves, the Hatters. She imagined the four glass sculptures related to each territory.

No one sat in the front-row seat in front of Sidney. As the noise of the crowd began to die down, Alice's eyes fell on the silent hostess standing near the sculptures. Her presence alone seemed to draw the attention and quiet reverence of everyone in the stadium.

She wore a black dress with gold trim, just like Crysta had worn in the waiting room, and she seemed to have Crysta's eyes. But the child had vanished, replaced by a striking woman with haunting, ethereal beauty.

"My fellow citizens of the nation, and territory leaders, I thank you for your hard work on this, the Survey Meeting!"

Her graceful voice echoed through the stadium, commanding the entire area. Alice shivered.

So Crysta was like the twins in Clover, and jumped between the form of a child and an adult. Alice filed that information away.

"It's been quite a while since the last meeting, and I'm sure there are many who have high expectations, hm? Those who amuse themselves with wagers are free to enjoy the Garden Party. However, keep in mind that any violence is *strictly* prohibited. I imagine there are many of you who are exhausted with all the fighting, so I want everyone to take advantage of this truce to refresh themselves and have a fabulous time!"

The queen ducked her head slightly, her voice turning more solemn. "And now…let the meeting begin!"

A tumult of cheers and horns exploded into the sky. As if following the noise, flights of doves flapped up into the atmosphere.

The queen smiled, clearly satisfied, and descended from the stage. She passed a Faceless announcer who climbed onto the stage and stood tall.

"Let's get this Survey Meeting underway!" he boomed. "Do those cheers mean that you're all ready for this?!"

As the announcer spoke, several dozen Faceless ascended the stage and began their work.

Alice squinted in confusion, not sure what was happening. Elliot seemed to notice.

"What're you doing?" he barked. "If you wanna see, look over there! That's where they calculate the territory size!"

"Where they… Oh!"

The diamond-shaped glass sculptures had been empty, but now they started to fill with sand in a slow trickle from overhead. Each vessel held a different color of sand: yellow, green, black, or blue. In the air in front of the sculptures, numbers ticked upward.

"What colors represent what territories?" Alice asked.

"Yellow's Diamond Castle," Dee answered. "Green's the Station."

"Then black is Gravekeeper, so blue's *us,* Big Sis."

The twins seemed on tenterhooks waiting for the results. Alice furrowed her brow.

"Really? The results of the Survey Meeting are decided in the sand?"

"Yup! Easy, right? Even the stupid rabbit can understand it with one look!"

"Ha ha, the dumb rabbit won't do anything hard. This way even *he* can see the results!"

"Are you little brats talking crap about me?!"

"Shut *up,*" Blood hissed. "If you're going to make noise, leave. Just go to the Garden Party and be done with it."

Dee whooped. "That's our Boss! He always knows what we want! See ya later!"

"Party, party! Free party!"

The twins clapped their hands excitedly and scrambled to get out. Blood sighed and flicked his blue-green gaze to Alice.

"They're surveying each territory for land mass, young lady—to use as the foundation for each team's power. You can leave if you want. I'll send someone for you when it's finished."

"Is that how it works?" Alice had assumed no one could leave until the meeting was over.

The Mad Hatter shrugged. "Sure. The other territory delegations are doing it."

Alice suddenly noticed that the territorial leaders *were* sitting alone. The rest of their Role-Holders had vanished already. The only exceptions were Sidney and Elliot.

"You won't be able to escape no matter where

you go, so do as you like."

Alice smiled sarcastically at him. *Implying that the guards are tracking me, huh?*

"Okay," she said slowly. "I've been wondering about the Garden Party, so I think I'll go there."

As she rose from her seat, she wondered if this was Blood trying to push her away. In the Country of Clover, Blood had a velvet tongue when it came to guiding Alice's actions. His words were smooth and effective.

It reminded her, once again, that the version of Blood who sat here with his legs crossed was a very different man. He kept his eyes on the sand towers and didn't spare her a glance.

She left him for the party.

The Survey Meeting ran a lot of other forms of entertainment—including the Garden Party, an impressive event packed with citizens eating, drinking, and laughing. Alice got to sample the best food in the country while listening unhurriedly to a live orchestra. By the time she returned to the stadium, the flows of sand were just cutting out.

The vessel with green sand seemed fuller than the others, so did that mean the Station's territory had the greatest land mass? The other three territories were locked with each other pretty closely.

It was time for the main event. Alice's heart started to pick up speed as she jogged to her seat. She wanted to see how the territory leaders "used their strengths."

The twins were already squirming by the time she got there. Blood, still sitting in the leader's seat, grinned up at her.

"Right on time. I was about to send someone after you."

"These are the numbers for each territory?"

"Yes. But it's just a *part* of each territory's score. The leaders can choose their own strengths and change the numbers from here on out." Blood pointed a gloved finger at Nightmare; the boyish Stationmaster had his hand on a small stand on his desk. Controls on the stand reacted to his hand movements.

The announcer leapt back on stage, riling up the crowd. "It's the moment you've all been waiting for!" he cried. "Will the Station keep its dominant place, or will the other leaders show their hidden hands?!"

Nightmare laughed, then coughed, then laughed again. He brimmed with youthful confidence.

"Ha! There's no doubt that I'll stay in the lead the entire time! What else...koff hack!" He curled over in a coughing fit, which made him seem less... threatening.

Jericho and then Crysta laid their hands on their stands, revealing some of their strength. Blood didn't move.

As the crowd roared around them, Blood raised an eyebrow at Alice. He beckoned her closer.

"How'd you like to give it a try, young lady?"

Alice had no idea what he was thinking; she quickly shook her head. "Thank you for the offer, but I must politely decline."

Blood laughed. He finally slid his hand onto the stand.

The stoppered blue sand started flowing into the

vessel once more. And in front of the sculpture, the floating numbers revolved and changed.

"......"

The majority of the people in the stadium held their breaths. Alice felt crushed by the pressure as she silently watched the progress. Beside her, the twins folded their hands together in desperate prayer.

The sand didn't fall at a constant speed—at times it would reduce to a tiny trickle, only to burst into a heavier flow. Alice guessed the flow rate was calculated to keep the spectators on the edges of their seats. *I bet it's driving the gamblers bananas.*

The flow of sand into the vessels slowed and finally stopped.

Cheers and miserable wails erupted simultaneously as the announcer, who had been silent up until this point, raised his voice to the crowd.

"And there you have it! The first-round victory goes to our hosts, Diamond Castle!"

The audience roared in response.

"And with that, the first Survey Meeting comes to a close! Don't miss the second round!"

As the announcer wrapped up the proceedings,

Crysta gave her hands a sharp clap. The Coliseum vanished around them, leaving everyone back in the waiting room they'd started in. The teleportation had been so smooth…almost as if the hands of a clock had been wound backwards.

Crysta puffed out her chest proudly at Sidney, who now stood beside her. "I hope you saw that," she chirped. "I'm the winner! Ha ha!"

His eyebrow twitched. "We have a veritable *mountain* of things to discuss, but this will suffice for now. I never thought you'd bring *that* out…"

"Rabbit, you're a rotten winner! You should be taking this opportunity to bury me in heaps of praise!"

Sidney heaved a great sigh as Crysta smiled innocently at him. Alice was starting to see that young, enthusiastic girl from earlier in this older, beautiful queen. It was a little unnerving.

On Alice's side of the room, Elliot was *livid.* His body trembled as his white fists clenched at his sides.

"I can't believe it… How could Blood *lose?!*"

Blood waved a hand. "Down, Elliot. The first round is always like this."

The final rankings for the round were Castle, Station, Grave/Museum, and Hatter Mansion in dead last. But Blood didn't seem bothered in the slightest. With Elliot practically shooting steam from his ears, Alice was confused as to who exactly had lost. Even the twins—who had been so caught up in their bets—just shrugged.

"Hm. So the Castle came in first this round… Kinda expected, but my winnings were crappy. How 'bout you, Brother?"

"Kinda like you. An' we were aimin' for the jackpot…"

Whatever payday Dee and Dum had been hoping for, this hadn't been it. The actual ranking of their *own* territory seemed irrelevant, though.

How very like them.

As Alice scanned the reactions of the other members in attendance, someone tapped on her shoulder.

"Yo. Good job today."

She craned her head to look behind her. "Jericho…?"

The Gravekeeper lifted a finger to his lips,

indicating for her to keep quiet. His eyes gleamed behind his glasses.

Fortunately, Elliot was still raging at the Survey Meeting results, so the Hatters were too distracted to look at Alice. She licked her lips and nodded.

"I wanted to apologize for my men," Jericho explained. "Earlier—in the street. I didn't have time for a proper apology in all the chaos."

"Don't worry about it. Actually, you *saved* me. Thank you for that."

She smiled and gave him a slight bow. A hint of pleasure played at the corners of his mouth.

"Still, my men started the whole thing. Maybe I can make it up to you at my place?"

"Your place? But your territory is…"

Her face broke into a grimace at the thought of the name *Gravekeeper,* but Jericho quickly waved away the idea with a flick of his hand.

"Now, wait—that's not what I mean. I wouldn't invite a lady to a *graveyard*. You may not know this, but I'm also the director of the art museum."

"Oh, right," she replied in relief. "I guess I *did* know that."

She'd heard about all the violent unrest in the Country of Diamonds, but she'd *also* been shut up in Hatter Mansion ever since arriving. She thought it might be nice to take a chance and get out a bit.

The territory leader runs the art museum. She was interested in what kind of art was on display there.

When she nodded, he handed her a slip of paper. It was a priority ticket with a fashionable design on it.

"Here. Come and enjoy yourself anytime you like."

"Thank you. I think I'll take you up on that."

Unfortunately, the Gravekeeper was a territory rival *and* ran an opposing Mafia organization. Alice didn't know if the Hatters would let her go, but she didn't receive many favors. She figured she'd take the ticket and be grateful.

A curious illustration of an animal printed on the ticket caught her eye. But when she squinted at it, Blood's voice drifted suddenly from much too close.

"Did you win a bet and you're checking your winnings, young lady?"

"B-Blood!"

Alice hurriedly stuffed the slip of paper into

her pocket. "N-no," she stuttered. "It's nothing." When she furtively glanced back at Jericho, she was relieved to see that he was already gone. She saw him in another area of the room, speaking to members of his territory.

Blood pursed his lips. "What is it? Did you have some business with someone?"

Blood seemed suspicious, but his eyes didn't move to Jericho. *Maybe he didn't put **that** much together,* Alice hoped.

"It's nothing," Alice repeated, then tried to change the subject. "What do we...do after this? Now that round one of the Survey Meeting is done?"

"We go home. The entertainment is over. The only question now is," Blood murmured, his eyes moving past her, "what do we do about *that?*"

Alice followed his gaze to see Elliot and the twins still making a fuss over the results. Well, to be more accurate—Elliot was furious and the twins added fuel to his fire.

"I just don't *get* it!" Elliot growled. "Blood was supposed to come in first, no matter what!"

"You're such an idiot!" Dee snapped back. "If

the boss wins every single time, what's the point of havin' a Survey Meeting at all?"

"Yeah, if everyone *knew* he was gonna win, we'd win even smaller pots! There's no money in the kitty if nobody's willin' to bet!"

"So? They can just bet on Blood!"

"......"

Their shouts carried through the waiting room, and Alice found herself grimacing. Elliot didn't seem to notice the other delegations making their exits nearby.

Blood sighed. "Shall we leave them behind?"

"It wouldn't be right, Blood."

He irritably waved a hand. "They're nothing but trouble."

As Alice hummed a noncommittal response, she slid her hand to the outside of her skirt pocket. Her fingers ran over the slight bump of the priority ticket inside.

ACT 3

The Unseen Relationship Chart

After the first Survey Meeting, things went back to normal in Hatter Mansion. Elliot, the twins, and most of the other mobsters went in and out of the place as they dealt with dangerous "jobs."

Still, it felt like the raids on the mansion had let up a bit. And when Alice was organizing the books in the reference library one time period, she asked her assistant maid a question about it—and received an unexpected reply.

"Well, sure~! Battles are basically banned during the entire time of the Survey Meeting~."

"Really? I heard fighting's prohibited *during* the meeting, but I thought that restriction only applied to the area around the Coliseum?"

"The Survey Meeting isn't like that~. Even if the first round is over, the second one will start up soon~. The Survey Meeting goes on until *all* rounds are over~."

"So one meet-up isn't the Survey Meeting—that's the collective name for all the meetings?"

In the Country of Hearts, the Ball had only lasted one night. But it was true that in the Country of Clover, the Assembly had occurred several times… maybe the Survey Meeting was more like that.

"You know how the Survey Meeting itself works now, right~?"

"More or less. The leaders of each territory choose one of five national forces and compare strengths."

"You got it~. In other words, the contest between the leaders is decided by the numbers, and if there's a battle, that *changes* the numbers. So if they kept fighting during the Survey Meeting, it wouldn't be an accurate survey~."

"Oh. That makes sense, I guess."

Alice knew the main reason for the "entertainment event" was to put people in close proximity for discussions. But the Survey Meeting was also a competition that pitted forces against forces—any fight between leaders would have a direct effect on the strength or size of those forces.

Especially with how violent people are in this world. She wouldn't put it past Elliot to raid the other territories if he thought it would help Blood win. And Dee and Dum would brave just about anything to increase their winnings.

Alice rose on her toes to slide a book onto a high shelf. But as she stretched her arm up, someone snatched the book out of her hand.

"Hey!"

"She's correct," Blood said evenly. "It's an *aggravating* rule, but it's still a rule. We can't ignore it."

Alice sighed and turned to the man, who flipped open the captured book.

This was another "fun" feature of the Survey Meeting—Blood was actually spending time in the reference library. He no longer just sent a servant. Alice was ready to suggest that he start doing that again to preserve more of his time.

"I asked you to gather some books for me last time period," he muttered as he flipped through the pages. "Where are they?"

"I put them in a pile here... Huh?"

Alice tilted her head in confusion. A pile of completely different books lay in the spot where she'd placed her own.

"Oh, those~? I took them with some other books to the warehouse~..."

"What?" Alice blurted.

The maid swiftly apologized. "I'll go get them now~," she declared as she rushed out of the room.

Alice was left alone with Blood. He glanced up from the pages to lock that blue-green gaze on her.

"I know you work hard here," he offered. "So I believe that *you* didn't misplace them. And if they were all together, the maid will probably find them quickly. Don't mind me—just go on with what you were doing."

Alice let out a breath. "Okay. But if you need anything, just ask me."

He hummed an affirmative.

Although she'd never said it to Blood directly, she

was really grateful to have the work of organizing the reference library. It housed a wide variety of tomes, including some blissful books from other collections that *weren't* about violence. Alice loved books and enjoyed the job.

The moment she started concentrating on her work, she stopped worrying about other eyes that could be in the room. This was a place where she could ignore the fact that she still lived under surveillance.

She was using a ladder to reach a high shelf—a crafts book hidden within the culture category—when Blood suddenly spoke again, reminding her he was in the room.

"Do you like books?" he asked simply.

"Hm? What did you say?"

As she descended the ladder to answer Blood's question, she realized that he had stopped reading the book in his hand at some point. His eyes were on her.

"I asked if you liked books. You seem to perk up when you're in this room."

Alice smiled. "Yeah. I enjoy organizing them, but

what I *really* love is reading."

She let one hand fondly trace down a book's spine. This particular bookshelf had been a disaster when she'd started—now it was neat and organized by title, with only a few empty spots.

She was living a life surrounded by books again. She never would've guessed that organizing and delivering books for a publishing house in her *old* world would come in handy in a place like Wonderland.

"You said you wanted to borrow a book before, young lady. Have you finished reading it?"

"Oh, you mean that misshelved mystery novel? I had it finished before my next work shift." She shrugged, but she heard her voice bounce a little. "I found the killer's trick predictable, but the detective had an interesting character and backstory."

Blood inhaled. After a long moment, he said, "But it wasn't enough for you."

"Huh?"

"It's written on your face. You wish I had a wider variety of books. Not satisfied with the selection in my house, hm?"

Alice furrowed her brow. "That's not what I mean. I just…"

She was organizing a reference library—not exactly the place for pleasure reading. And even though she received a more than decent salary for it, she was also working for a Mafia organization in the middle of a turf war. It wasn't like she could leave and pop over to town to buy some pleasure reading, like she'd done when working at Heart Castle.

"You let me read whatever I want here, and I like the job. Besides, I've never been picky about genre—I can enjoy whatever books are in front of me."

As Blood stared at her, she superimposed a memory of the old Blood over him. Books in this world always made her think of Blood in the Countries of Hearts and Clover. He'd always recommended and lent books to her, to read between work shifts at Heart Castle. He usually handed her books about tea or roses, granted, since they seemed to be his biggest hobbies—they weren't as formal as technical manuals, but she learned a lot of new things from them. Even if they were (probably) part of his strategy to manipulate her.

That was always a little frustrating, but she liked aspects of it. A little nonfiction was good for the soul. And learning about what he loved was like learning more about *him*.

She liked that memory.

"When I think you're coming," he would say, *"I find myself wondering what book is worth choosing for you. I'm just happy for the distraction."*

They'd both been busy people in Hearts and Clover, but they'd always maintained an oddly unhurried relationship. They'd never been apart for long. Considering he was a fearsome Mafia boss and she was a powerless Outsider, she imagined they made an odd pair.

And probably still did in Diamonds.

"If there's any book you want," Blood said at last, turning back to the tome in his hands, "just tell me. You work hard and you have decent taste. Just tell the maid, and I'll see if we can get it."

That took Alice by surprise. "Uh…what?" she blurted. "But this is a reference library. I can't just order things that I think are *fun*."

"It doesn't have to be for here—we can leave it in your room. I'm sure you have space there for some books."

"Well, yeah, but…are you sure?"

She was *slightly* more welcome in the mansion now, but that didn't make her a pampered guest. And she didn't know if she'd suddenly vanish from Diamonds someday, just as fast as she'd appeared—so she didn't keep many personal possessions. Had Blood noticed that?

"You're living and working in my house, and *I* don't care if you have a few books in your room. You've barely touched your salary, so you can use that to pay for them."

Alice frowned. "You've kept good tabs on me."

"All you talk about in this library is work," he murmured, a teasing edge to the words. "It's a shame."

Alice rolled her eyes to the ceiling. *How could I forget what kind of man this is?* she mused. Watching her from the shadows, cutting in with surprising insight. That level of intelligence fueled his bad attitude, after all.

"You don't dress up like other girls your age," he

went on. "And you don't spend money on hobbies. It isn't hard to figure out that you don't know what to do with the money you've made so far." He shrugged. "If you don't feel any material desires, there's nothing I can suggest. It's just not a bad thing to invest yourself where your interests lie."

"……"

Alice was surprised at how much he was pushing it. She hadn't expected Diamonds Blood to talk like that, considering they weren't exactly friends here. Maybe they were finally shedding the cold formality between a boss and subordinate.

After a moment of silence, she nodded. "Okay. Um…thank you."

"I didn't do anything worth thanks."

He hadn't turned his eyes up from the book in his hands. She cleared her throat.

"Should you really be here?"

"Yes. If I take the book with me, it's a pain to return it afterwards. I just needed to quickly check something."

"Oh. Uh…" While Alice tried to formulate an answer, Blood slid the book back onto the shelf and grabbed another. He picked book after book and flipped through the pages.

He was head of the Hatter Family. He could just send a servant to the library to fetch a book, and then send the servant back to return it. So Alice figured he had other reasons for coming.

Still, his attitude and behavior baffled her. Even if the Blood in the other countries had liked her, she knew, all self-deprecation aside, that Diamonds Blood saw her as a friend *at best*.

"......"

Maybe there was some good to being in Diamonds, after all. She'd stopped constantly wishing she was back in the Country of Hearts.

I can never...make up my mind. Do I even want to go back now?

The memory of Blood in the other countries remained vivid in the back of her mind. He'd invited her to the tiny rose garden in so many night periods. He'd always pushed her to leave the castle and move in with him.

It had probably just been lip service at the time, but that had been his version of courtesy. After all, no member of the Mafia, let alone a boss, would be so welcoming of someone who was nothing more than an Outsider.

But Alice had always refused. She'd never felt that the Hatter Mansion was "her place" in the world, so she always answered the same way.

She watched the profile of the man reading a book nearby. Even if she'd accepted the invitation of the old Blood, that would have meant living with the old Blood. Not *this* Blood.

What kind of relationship *did* she want with this Blood? She pursed her lips and turned back to her bookshelves.

She lost her train of thought when she suddenly noticed the mess before her. She groaned aloud. "Not again."

"Is something wrong?" Blood asked.

"I had this whole shelf perfectly arranged two time periods ago. But someone already messed it up!"

Blood walked up behind Alice and peered over her shoulder. She tried not to be self-conscious at the warm presence looming over her.

She swallowed and pointed toward a book's spine. "See?" she asked. "This shelf's supposed to be for books on construction materials. So what the heck is this?" She plucked the offending book from the shelf and furrowed her brow at the large image of a castle stamped on the red leather binding. "I guess the maid only looked at the cover when she put it away—"

"Wait," Blood interjected. "I was just wondering where I put that. It was *there?*" To Alice's surprise, a small, nostalgic smile flitted across Blood's face.

She blinked at him. "This book is yours?"

"Yes. *I* own it—not the Family. I assume the maid accidentally added it to her stack when she was collecting reference books to return. I guess she stuck it here… Oh. That book over there is mine, too."

His gloved hands gestured toward a bookshelf. About half the books were lined up on the shelf, but in seemingly random order. Alice's eye twitched.

Her hand automatically went to pull the new book he pointed at, but then she stopped herself. "Wait. You mean this one?"

It had a familiar title; she even remembered the

author's name. She opened the cover and looked at a number of pages.

She *did* know this one. She'd borrowed this very same book in the Country of Clover from Blood.

"What's wrong with it?" he asked.

"Nothing," she answered quickly. "Uh…yeah. Do you want me to have your books delivered to your room?" She'd been to his bedroom in the other countries plenty of times and knew he had massive bookshelves in there.

Blood shot her a dubious expression, but it quickly vanished from his face. "Sure. You can bring them to my room later."

"Uh… You want *me* to bring them?" She hadn't been in his Diamonds room yet; she wasn't sure she was allowed there. "Are you sure?"

He raised an eyebrow. "Yes, I'm sure."

Alice opened her mouth, then closed it. "Okay, then."

And with that, he turned to leave. "I imagine the maid will be back soon," he called over his shoulder. "Bring those books I ordered with you when you deliver mine."

Alice once again asked if he was sure, and Blood waved a confirming hand as he exited the room. No more than a few moments later, the maid returned through a different door.

"Sorry for the wait~!"

Alice took a long breath. She carefully finished collecting her research material, tucked it in a file, and piled it with Blood's books. She clutched everything to her chest and stepped into the hallway.

This Hatter Mansion had the same general layout as in Hearts and Clover; she walked the familiar corridors, enduring wary gazes from the Diamonds mobsters. But none of them stopped her beeline for Blood's room.

Two guards stood at the door. She cleared her throat.

"Blood asked me to deliver these… Can I come in?"

"Of course~. Step right in~."

Alice's hands were full, but one of the Family mobsters opened the door for her. He waved her in.

"……"

The room hadn't changed much between

countries; she felt a rush of feelings well up in her heart. Nostalgia, relief...even a little discomfort.

An uncharacteristically big mess of papers and books covered his desk, in front of a wall of bookshelves stuffed with tomes stacked sideways or perched precariously. She didn't smell the familiar, soothing scent of roses and hot tea.

Now she saw why the disorganized reference library hadn't really fazed him. *He* was a bit of a mess. Blood shuffled through papers at the desk and glanced up as she stepped in.

"That was quicker than I thought," he murmured. "I'm glad you're so dedicated."

"Well, I don't have much to do other than my job." She gestured to her books. "Where should I put the reference stuff?"

"On the table over there is fine."

He pointed his pen at a coffee table between two couches used for meetings. Alice placed the folder on the edge of the table and held up his personal books.

"And where should I put these?"

"Wherever. Up to you."

"......"

Is he busy? I expected him to have more opinions.

She headed to the messy bookshelf. Since most people organized their bookshelves by author or genre or something, she assumed he had a system. She wouldn't let the chaos of the reference library spread to his personal space…especially since this was a much smaller job.

She slid the first book onto the shelf in its apparent space, righting and correcting the books around it. Then she moved around to place the others.

"Um… This would be landscaping, and this is…"

Alice moved left and right across the bookshelves that lined the walls. As she tucked the final book—a detective novel—into its space, she puffed out a sigh and tilted her eyes up.

The shelf right above eyeline held a full row of children's books. While she scanned the titles, her hands slowly dropped to her sides.

She recognized a series of five books in the corner bookshelf. But counting the volumes again, she found something puzzling.

"These books…"

Just like the book in the reference library, these

were tomes that Blood had lent her in the Country of Clover. But in Alice's memory, there were only *three* in the series. Alice had assumed Diamonds was a country stuck in the past, even if it wasn't a completely perfect version of the past…so the two extra spines confused her.

"Is there something about those books that interests you?" Blood asked from behind her.

"I…guess you could say that."

"Then take them."

"Really?"

"Yes." She heard his papers shuffling as his voice took on a hint of disgust. "No one loves reading more than I do, but I'm all tied up with the Survey Meeting right now."

Alice brightened. "Thanks! Do you mind if I borrow all five books?"

"Go ahead."

As Alice pulled the series from the shelf, she double-checked the titles and authors against what she remembered. *Yeah, this is it.*

She hugged the books to her chest, slightly irritated. She'd be leaving with as many books as she'd come with.

When she turned back to him, he was still buried in some document. "From what I hear," he murmured, "you hardly ever leave the mansion. Would you be interested in some entertainment?"

"Well, it isn't so much that I don't leave, but that it's *hard* to leave... Oh. Yeah, I would."

Was he teasing her? Still, she instinctively slid one hand into her pocket to run her fingers over Jericho's ticket. She figured that if any of the servants found it, she'd come under even more suspicion, so she always kept it on her.

She'd made a promise never to leave the mansion without Blood's permission, but since she didn't intend to run or spill the place's secrets, she was getting a little sick of being suspected for no reason. She didn't get to talk to Blood in private much, so she figured she'd take a chance. She cleared her throat.

"Say, Blood...the next time I have a day off, would you mind if I went to the art museum?"

"Hn. The art museum...?"

Maybe he didn't expect the question, but he

looked up from his documents with a wicked smile on his face. The nib of his pen tapped the paper over and over.

"You've already seduced the Gravekeeper?" he drawled. "Rumor has it that everyone loves an Outsider, but I think you also have a *knack* for using your charms." *Tap tap* went the pen. "I can't say I approve of your tastes, though. He's already a dead man."

Alice blinked. "A dead man?" she repeated, her stomach tightening in discomfort.

Blood leaned back in his chair. "If you really want to go, I won't stop you. But if you manage to romance any good information out of the Gravekeeper, pass it on to your boss, will you?"

Alice furrowed her brow. "Please don't make assumptions like that. And...I should get back to work."

She didn't like his answer, but it *did* seem like permission. *I'll take it,* she thought.

Alice turned and left the room. Blood said nothing as the door shut behind her.

Alice spent some quality time in her room, splayed out on her stomach on her bed. She voraciously plowed through the books Blood had lent her.

She was already coming toward the end of the third book, but her heart filled with doubts. "There are different plot twists here," she complained aloud. "When I first read it, this monk character wasn't in it."

It was a tale of a traveling group, and as far as Alice remembered, the main character had five companions. But by the end of the third book, one more had joined them: a monk. The group still had the same purpose for the journey, and all of the other companions and their backgrounds were the same… there was just a monk now. It confused her.

"……"

She finally finished the third book. As she put it down and reached for the fourth, her hand stopped. It slowly slid back to the sheets.

She sighed and closed her eyes. "It's kinda like me as I am now," she muttered. *A completely unknown person joining a group.*

The books even had plot developments that Alice had never read before, and of course, there were two extra volumes. Alice had stronger and stronger doubts about the books' very existence.

*Then Diamonds **isn't** just a past version of the world I knew.*

"If it has a different beginning," she mused, "then of course it'll have a different ending. But that's not very…satisfying."

If Peter hadn't pulled her into the Country of Hearts first, then Alice would have had a very different point of view on the Country of Diamonds. The Hatter Family wasn't as mature an organization; with such short-tempered thugs, Alice probably never would've chosen to stay there. Alice was, after all, a realist—she tried to protect herself from dangerous situations.

"I first thought Wonderland was a dream, and that drove my attitude. But now with everyone against me, I doubt I could even *fake* that attitude."

Without any attachments or friendship, she might have just passed Hatter Mansion and kept going.

Thinking that, she let out a sardonic laugh.

"Maybe I wished for something *different*."

Maybe somewhere in Alice's heart, she'd wanted to build a different relationship with the people of Wonderland—something distinct from what she'd had in the Countries of Hearts and Clover. She knew worrying about it wouldn't help, but the thought kept whirling around and around in her mind.

Like the spinning hands of a clock. She shook her head to clear it and rose from the bed.

She'd already decided to take Jericho up on his invitation and go to the art museum during the next time period. She guessed a Hatter guard or two would probably follow her there, since they still didn't seem to really trust her. Their organization was still building its forces and clearly hated taking chances.

The downside of being a young, female Outsider around insecure mobsters.

She wanted a change of pace, so she left her room and ducked outside for a walk within the mansion grounds. As usual, she cut through the other Faceless wandering around, their eyes burning holes in her back.

"Good evening~," one of them called, his voice careful. "Out for a walk~?"

"Good evening," Alice replied politely. "Are you guys on patrol?"

"Yes, night patrol~. It's such a pain, huh~?"

"It's hard to find intruders when they use the cover of night~."

She knew they were under pressure to watch her, so she couldn't exactly blame them…but she wanted some space. Alice made for a place she knew would be more-or-less deserted.

As she traveled deeper into the mansion's outdoor grounds, the weeds grew thicker under her feet; she tried not to trip on them. A bird hooted somewhere nearby.

Was that an owl? Alice followed the sound to the trees, curiosity compelling her.

In the shadow of a tree, she saw a human shape that didn't look like a Hatter Faceless. The dappled moonlight played on his white suit jacket.

"…Blood?"

She squinted; the person vanished into the trees.

Had that been him? She followed the shadow.

She figured that if this place were forbidden to her, someone would've tried to stop her—like earlier. But no one had said a thing. She took a breath and ducked under an overhanging branch.

As she followed the white shadow deeper into the deserted area, Alice started to hatch a theory about where Blood might go. She didn't know if the secret rose garden existed in Diamonds or not, but that place only admitted the few people who knew of it. Even *Elliot* had never been in the place. Blood had always saved it for himself, his sister…and Alice, whom he'd invited on a whim.

She hiked through the woodsy grounds, but couldn't catch sight of Blood's trail. She wrinkled her nose.

"I was sure it was this way…"

Maybe it was her own fault for letting him disappear. She glanced right and left, ignoring her feet until they suddenly rammed into something.

"Aagh!"

By the time she realized that someone had tripped her, she was spilling toward the ground. A rock-hard hand gripped her arm, yanked her up, and shoved

her against a tree.

"B-Blood, what are you—"

Blood abruptly pinned her wrists above her head. His other hand shoved his cane against her throat.

"Didn't anybody tell you this area is off-limits?" he hissed. "I stayed quiet and followed you, and I was *thrilled* to have finally uncovered your assassination plot...but here you are, unarmed as usual."

Alice choked. "Assassination plot? I don't know what you're talking about!"

"Decent ladies don't chase men in the dark."

"N-no, I was just..." She tried to swallow against the rod rammed up under her chin. "Whatever I did, I don't deserve *this!*"

Maybe he wasn't as bad as Elliot, but Blood in the Country of Diamonds wasn't a patient man. She stared at him, imploring him to at least lower the weapon, but he only gave her a short, nasal laugh.

"If this is your idea of a come-on, you should try whatever you used to seduce the Gravekeeper on me. That sounds more *fun.*" His lips curled. "But not in the woods. I like my women in my room."

"......"

The cane dragged from her throat and started to trace the line of her body over her clothes. She felt less sexually threatened and more in danger of *him killing her* as he whispered in her ear, "Or maybe you *like* this kind of action."

His low voice sent ice down her spine. This man acted on whims. That could make him do *anything*.

She cringed from the lips in her ear. "Stop it!" she cried. "I only thought you were going to the secret garden!"

Blood went silent as death.

He pulled back, his hand still gripping her wrists. Any expression on his face had disappeared, but something severe shone in his blue-green eyes.

Hostility.

That gaze pierced through Alice's body and cut into her heart. She was terrified that she'd said too much.

Blood had told her how he'd kept his garden secret—he'd murdered the builders outside the mansion grounds, then created a hard and fast rule that no one was to enter the area without his permission. The only people who knew it existed were the only people allowed in.

And Blood in the Country of Diamonds had never told her about the garden.

She could barely breathe as he stared at her with murder in his eyes.

"You," he said, his voice razor-sharp and very, very cold. "What do you know?"

Alice tried to calm her pounding heart. Blood wouldn't kill her yet. If she had information that he wanted, that had to come first.

She stared, morbidly fascinated, at the man who loomed over her. She didn't know why she did that, when he could kill her right then and there.

His eyes, violent and disturbed, sparkled in the night gloom. He was *interested* in her. And in the intensity of that gaze, something deep in her chest clamored for her attention.

It wasn't fear. Alice chewed on her lip as that sensation throbbed in her heart.

What's happening to me? she thought in a panic. *Am I crazy? He thinks I'm an enemy!*

Was it that she'd become far too familiar with the insanity of Wonderland? She honestly didn't know. After a moment of thought, the words came smoother than expected.

"If you want to know something," she told him, "then do your research. Or is it too hard for a Mafia boss to investigate one little Outsider girl…?"

She knew it was provocative. But she didn't want to be the only one trembling.

"……"

"……"

She felt locked in a staring match as the silence dragged on. But the bitter cold between them finally drained away.

He released her wrists and took a breath.

She still sensed animosity as she slowly lowered her hands. But the threat in his voice had blurred together with an emotion she hadn't seen in him before.

"I guess that's true," he murmured. "I see the value in investigating you. I'll expose whatever truths you're hiding."

"I…look forward to what you find out."

The words that tumbled out of her taunted him, but she was still confused about her own feelings.

This wouldn't have worked on the old Blood. He would've *never* risen to such a cheap provocation from a teenage girl.

But it *had* worked. And Alice had an idea of what was coming next.

The question was, if it went as Alice thought, would she be happy or sad about it? What did these two Bloods have in common? How were they *different?* Her feelings toward them were so complicated she couldn't explain it if she tried.

"Come to the secret garden whenever you like," the old Blood had said. *"My word is law here, and I say you can visit anytime the mood strikes you."*

The secret rose garden at night. She'd managed to gain access to his hard-won sanctuary...

But this place wasn't his. It belonged to a different Blood Dupre.

ACT 4

At the Museum

Alice took another step down the street, letting out a long breath. Her shoes tapped on the concrete.

Here we go.

With the exception of the Survey Meeting, this was the first time she'd left Hatter territory. Supposedly Diamonds was more violent than the countries of Hearts and Clover; fortunately, she hadn't run into any serious trouble. Yet.

She knew a graveyard and a museum lay in the territory of the Gravekeeper, but had no idea where to find Jericho himself. She flagged down two men walking nearby.

"Um, excuse me. I-I came to see the leader?"

She couldn't decide whether to call him the Gravekeeper or the museum curator, so she stuck to vague language. One of the men seemed to understand her, though.

"Someone from outside the territory has come to see Jericho? That's unusual."

"I saw him headed toward the graveyard a little while ago," the other man said. "So he's probably still there. Just head straight down this road."

The first man frowned. "But it's probably not worth going," he warned. "Jericho's a busy man, y'know? Nobody ever really knows where he goes or when he leaves."

"In the graveyard," Alice repeated. "Okay. Thank you!"

She continued on with mixed feelings. For a moment she thought of waiting for him at the museum, but if he was that busy—and it made sense, if he had three huge responsibilities—they could easily miss each other.

As she headed down the street toward the graveyard, the Faceless around her thinned out. She saw several men who had stopped to have a chat a little farther down the road. Most of them wore suits, but one of them carried a shovel.

As Alice approached, the man with the shovel turned to her. He blinked.

"Oh! It's you."

Alice stopped. "Huh? Have we met before?"

She'd never been in this territory before; how could someone know her? Had he seen her during the Survey Meeting?

"I heard that, um, the Gravekeeper Jericho might be at the graveyard… Is he still there?"

The man stared at her in surprise. His stern face had opened in confusion.

"Huh?"

Alice didn't know what the problem was. "Like I said—someone said he went this way, so I was wondering if Jericho was here. If he's too busy, I can come back later."

"Heh. Heh heh."

"Ha ha ha!"

The group of men tried to suppress their chuckles and failed. When she just stared at them expectantly, they burst into raucous laughter.

The man with the shovel seemed the most amused. He held his stomach in a loud belly laugh.

"Ha ha ha ha! I'm impressed!" he boomed. "That's the first time anyone's said that to my face!"

"Boss," one of the other men said, flicking an almost sympathetic look at Alice. "You shouldn't say that to the poor girl!"

"You're right. I can't blame her when she isn't used to it… Ha ha!"

Alice scowled, not sure if they were making fun of her. The man with the shovel eventually wiped his eyes and leaned closer to her, grinning.

"You really don't recognize me?"

"Recognize you from… Huh?"

He closed his handsome face into a familiar, calm expression, and Alice suddenly noticed the scars. The scars that usually melted from people in Wonderland.

Alice gasped. "Wait… Are *you* Jericho?!"

He looked completely different. His suit and glasses were gone, replaced with rough outdoor clothes, heavy workman's boots, and a pair of goggles hanging around his neck. She noticed a bird pin attached to his jacket…was that the same one he'd worn during the Survey Meeting?

Jericho stroked his jaw and flashed a wry smile.

"I'm sorry I laughed at you. But I expected you to recognize me from *this* close."

"No, I should be the one to apologize! The atmosphere here is so different, I didn't realize it was you…"

"No harm done. This is what the Gravekeeper wears when he does his job."

Alice was embarrassed, but the man seemed completely at ease. Just as warm as when she'd first met him.

She smiled back, feeling reeled in. She slowly drew the ticket from her pocket.

"Thanks for the priority ticket. I was hoping you could show me the art museum."

"Is that right? I'm sorry… After coming all the way to my territory, you've had to take the long way around." Jericho shook his head; the men behind him started to speak.

"Don't worry, Boss—we can handle things here. Take the young lady where she wants to go."

"We can make the rounds ourselves. Besides, isn't it

on your schedule to return to the museum about now?"

To emphasize their arguments, they all gave him farewell waves. Jericho smiled weakly.

"Then I'll leave it to you guys. Contact me if there are any problems."

"Got it. Bye, Boss!"

Alice tried to say something, but the men quickly shuffled away. She looked up at Jericho.

"Are you sure about this? I only came here to thank you—I didn't mean to interfere."

"You heard them—it's about time I returned to the museum, anyway."

Alice admired his casual kindness. After so much time with the restless Diamonds Hatters, Jericho's mature attitude was refreshing.

"Okay. Um, thanks."

Jericho didn't take her hand; he just walked a few steps in front of her, turned, and smiled.

"Let's go."

They arrived at the museum in no time. Unfortunately, a huge crowd had lined up at the turnstiles. As she gripped her ticket and prepared for the wait, she looked up at Jericho.

And froze.

He seemed *completely different* again. If she hadn't just been talking to him, she would've assumed this was a different man.

He answered her unasked question. "We've changed venues. I have to dress accordingly."

He'd worn a black suit for the Survey Meeting and blue-collar work clothes as the Gravekeeper— now, as the museum's curator, the only thing his outfit shared with those two was the opening at the chest. He wore an unimposing, light brown coat and pants, his delicate spectacles resting on his nose once more.

Other than the scars, he looked like a scholar. *Fitting*.

He smiled. "You'll get used to me soon enough. Now come over here—I'll guide you."

Alice frowned. "I'd feel bad cutting in line."

Jericho laughed. "That's what a priority ticket is for!"

He beckoned her to join him. They walked alongside the line, she handed her ticket over at the turnstile, and they squeezed into the packed museum.

Alice paused in the front room, her eyes widening. Other attendees bustled past her.

The paintings on the walls were *alive*.

Painted elks ran through fields of swaying grass, fish splashed in two-dimensional streams. A bird swooped *out of a painting* and flapped through the room, causing a few children nearby to clap their hands in delight.

"This…this is amazing," Alice breathed. "What *is* all this? How is it happening?!"

"If I told you the trick, it wouldn't be interesting to you anymore. Besides—we're only getting started."

Alice felt like she'd stepped into another dimension. It wasn't just that animals could leap out of their picture frames—the pictures lit up, featured shifting clouds, flickered with geometric patterns. Alice found herself squinting at the red glow emanating from the painting of a sunset. The beauty moved her. She knew it had to be some sort of illusion, but it still gripped her and wouldn't let go.

A rabbit jumped out of a painting and bounced past Alice. She watched it run, dumbfounded.

"Mommy!" some kid shouted as she pointed at it. "It's a bunny rabbit! Let's catch it together!"

"Whoa!" someone else cried. "Did a flying squirrel just jump up there?"

Alice rubbed her eyes. "I still want to know the trick behind it," she murmured.

Jericho gave a wry smile. "You came all the way here—take your time and enjoy the exhibits. You can have all the explanations you want later."

"Thank you. But do you really have time to be my guide? You seem so busy…"

Skipping the line with her priority ticket had been enough of a blessing. She didn't want to monopolize the time of the most important man in the museum.

But Jericho pursed his lips. "No, I'll stay. Right now, I'm more concerned…about *you* than anything else that may come up."

"Me? Why are you concerned about me?" She and Jericho had hardly spoken; she wondered what might make him worry about her. She glanced in a nearby mirror to confirm that she didn't look sick or anything.

Jericho's reflection loomed behind hers. He gazed through his glasses at Alice's reflection in the mirror.

"You don't look satisfied," he said evenly. "Something's wrong."

"It's not that…"

"It *is* that. And it concerns me." His eyes were unreadable. "Did something happen to you in Hatter Mansion?"

"Nothing specific." Alice's lips moved as if she were talking to herself in the mirror. She pushed her shoulders back, feeling a rare opportunity.

"Jericho…I've just been wondering. Why did the move bring me to the Country of Diamonds? Why *here?* I can't get the question out of my mind."

She'd never been able to say those words to anyone in Hatter Mansion. Jericho raised his eyebrows in response.

"Then…before you came here, you were in another country?"

Alice nodded. "But if I say more, it'll only be

complaints. You don't want to hear that." Alice didn't like subjecting others to her grousing.

The curator in the mirror puffed out a breath. "I don't mind. And I don't know what you've heard, but…I'm living on dead time."

Alice remembered a similar comment from Blood. "Dead time?" she repeated. "What does that mean? You're alive!"

The people of Wonderland were living embodiments of time. It was why when one person vanished, another quickly came in to take his place. Everyone in Wonderland said the same thing: *We're replaceable. Life and death are cheap.*

But this was the first time someone had said he was *already* dead.

Jericho stood there for a long moment, a fragile smile on his face. Then he tapped his chest…maybe referencing the clock inside.

"Don't worry about it," he said quietly. "This is the Gravekeeper's territory—I take care of the graves, both below and above."

"……"

She still didn't understand the "already dead"

thing, but it didn't sound like Jericho would elaborate. And she was pretty desperate to talk to someone about her situation, so if he was offering...

"Well, I first came to the Country of Hearts," she explained. "I stayed in Heart Castle as a maid, sorta. Then I moved into the Country of Clover. I knew there was infighting between the different territories, but I still visited a lot of the other ones—including Hatter Mansion."

As Alice talked, Jericho listened quietly. She cleared her throat.

"When I came to Diamonds, I went to Hatter Mansion again. And the same people live there, but...they don't recognize me anymore. And little by little, I've realized that I never *existed* in this place before."

"Same people?" Jericho repeated.

Alice ran her finger down the mirror. It left an oily mark from her skin, which quickly vanished.

"I knew Blood, Elliot, Dee, and Dum in Hearts and Clover. And even if they didn't recognize me, I figured it was safer to stay somewhere *I* knew. But now that I've been there awhile...I'm not sure that impulse decision was a good one. I feel a little stuck now."

If she'd gone to other territories and investigated them instead, or even if she'd been honest about where she'd come from the first time she re-met Blood, maybe things would've gone differently. Maybe they would've gone *better*.

She knew what-ifs wouldn't help her, but she couldn't get them out of her head. Did she regret her decision? Something squeezed in her chest.

"This place may be a 'past' version of the countries I lived in," she offered. "Maybe not a pure version of the past, but *some* kind of earlier version. Maybe that's why the people of the Country of Diamonds aren't the people I know. I realize that, and still…"

It was hard to think of everyone in Hatter Mansion as the people she once knew. They were so different now. Even if the twins hadn't changed much deep down, they spent all their time as adults. She couldn't get used to Elliot glaring at her in suspicion. And the way Blood treated her…that was a whole issue in itself.

"How were you involved with the Hatters and the

people in other countries?" Jericho suddenly asked.

"They were all friends of mine. At least, I'd like to think so. And that didn't change in the move from Hearts to Clover."

She conjured up memories that made her heart ache. The twins getting her tangled up in their dangerous pastimes, sometimes bringing along Boris—who they considered a friend—for fun. Or running around with Gowland and Pierce, or visiting an amusement park that didn't exist in this country...

Elliot had pointed a gun at her when they'd first met, too. But he'd swiftly dropped that animosity and treated her to his weird carrot cooking. She and Elliot had been *friends*.

She wasn't sure how long she stood there, but Jericho opened his mouth to break the silence. "Then you got along well with the Mad Hatter himself?" he clarified.

"Yeah. We were really...close." She flashed back to his secret rose garden.

Jericho's eyes widened. "Really?"

"I was a little surprised we became friends, too. He seemed like a difficult guy. But we're both big readers, so we connected over that—he'd recommend books and lend them to me. If I went to the mansion, he would pretty much always invite me to a tea party… Oh, and if it was a nighttime period, he'd give me a guided tour of Hatter Mansion."

She'd often asked Blood if he should be so attentive to a wandering Outsider not attached to his territories. But Blood answered her every time with a smile playing on his lips:

*"It's just a whim. And if you spilled my secrets, it would only lead to **different** fun."*

The way he said it always sent a chill down her spine. He was a nasty man, and she wasn't stupid enough to test him.

Back in her old world, she never would've gotten involved with a Mafia boss…but she'd been bold when she'd thought Wonderland was a dream. She'd visited him over and over. And his special treatment surprised her, especially with the secret rose garden. He'd accepted her, right? Even if he was so guarded about his feelings?

That Blood accepted me, anyway.

She tried to remind herself that it had taken a long

time to foster her relationships in Hearts and Clover. She hadn't been in Diamonds long, so it made sense that she was still struggling.

She sighed. "It's not like I *want* to get that close to the Blood in Diamonds. He's similar here, but not the same person. And so much of our first relationship was based on lucky circumstances—I doubt I'll have a repeat of that stuff."

"Then what relationship *do* you want with him now?" Jericho asked softly.

For a moment, Alice said nothing. She'd been asking herself the same question for a long time.

"I...don't know," she answered at last. "But I get the feeling that we don't know enough about each other, even though we're under the same roof—and that's a problem. I'd like to at least get to *know* Blood of the Country of Diamonds."

She'd stopped longing constantly for Hearts and Clover. She was ready to dig into Diamonds—and she had a burning desire to re-learn these people she once knew.

Jericho suddenly chuckled. She furrowed her brow at him.

"What?"

"Sorry, sorry. I wasn't making fun of you. I just think *you're* the one person who could pull that off."

She eyed him suspiciously. "Hard to believe that when you're laughing."

The man's face, reflected in the mirror, swiveled around. When Alice turned from the mirror to look up at him, he rested his large hand on her head and mussed her hair.

"I mean it. I don't know the Mad Hatter very well myself, but I figured you'd be okay under his care. Otherwise I would've invited you to live with me." He flashed a warm smile. "Although I'm starting to regret that I didn't offer."

Alice paused at that. "Okay under his care?" she repeated at last. "But I told you—I had a relationship with a *different* Blood." The imperturbable, dominating Blood of Hearts and Clover. The mature Mafia boss.

Diamonds Blood wasn't nearly that secure.

"But aren't both Mad Hatters the same at heart? I wonder if it's something to get so upset about."

"This Blood doesn't take me seriously. I'm not

sure I *can* be friends with him."

"But you made friends with the Mad Hatters of the *other* countries." He waved a hand. "You'll be fine—we're all connected to our other selves. The location, what comes before or after... None of those things make much difference."

Confused, Alice ran her fingers through her hair to comb it back. But the museum curator just let out a final, clear laugh.

"Maybe the Mad Hatter *you* knew was the type to twist you around his little finger," he pointed out. "But the Hatter here is still young. You should try to turn the tables on him."

"......"

How was she supposed to turn the tables on a man that dangerous? He'd already accused her of being an assassin just for following him into a garden!

Arguments bubbled up her throat, but they died when she looked into Jericho's face. She closed her mouth.

His words were the first real *help* she'd been offered in Diamonds. She didn't want to just throw that out.

So she slowly nodded, wondering if she could take his advice.

After returning from the art museum, Alice went back to her room to prepare for work. The library maid appeared almost immediately, as if sensing Alice's presence.

"Orders from the boss~," she said. "He wanted you to visit his room as soon as you were back~."

"But I'm supposed to start work—"

"Boss made it clear that this comes first~. Please go to the boss's room, okay~?"

Alice grimaced. She wasn't a Hatter, so she didn't technically need to listen to him…but it would be stupid to ignore an egotistical mobster who had cornered her with a crony. She didn't want grudges later.

Alice gave a reluctant nod. "Blood first, then straight to work. Do you mind starting without me?"

"Not at all~. See you soon~!" The maid bowed and breezed out, cool as you please.

When Alice arrived at Blood's room, she saw the usual Faceless guards standing outside the doors. She took a breath.

"I heard that Blood called for me. Can I go in?"

"Oh, it's you~." One of the guards casually knocked on the door. "Boss, she's here~."

"Send her in."

The two guards stood aside. Alice pushed through the door.

Blood sat behind his desk, seemingly buried in more paperwork. He didn't even look up when she walked in.

"Did you enjoy the art museum?" he asked coolly. "Did the Gravekeeper allow any information to slip?"

Alice scowled. "If you wanted a spy, you shouldn't have sent a librarian."

His lips curled at the snub. "Then you're not interested in changing jobs. Too bad—I'd be happy to make you an intelligence officer."

"It doesn't look like you have time to jerk me around right now."

Blood finally dropped the papers in his hands and sighed. His lifted his blue-green gaze.

"I'm busy—our organization is new. Anyway, have a seat. Some rare tea just came in, so I thought I'd forgo the sweets and listen to your stories of the museum instead."

"Uh...I didn't see anything that special." Although not strictly true, considering the paintings were *magic,* she assumed Blood already knew that about his enemy's territory.

Alice shot him a suspicious look, but she could tell he wasn't going to let her go until they'd gone over what he was interested in. She lowered herself onto the red sofa.

Blood grabbed a bell and rang it once; a maid appeared in the room seconds later.

"You rang~?"

"I'd like tea. The leaves should be... Hm. What would be best?"

Then he hadn't actually *decided* on the tea. Seeing Blood rest his chin on his hands in thought, Alice cut in.

"Maybe you wouldn't mind if I chose the tea?"

"Oh ho? You?"

"Yeah. If my conversation's taking the place of

sweets, then I would know what kind of tea goes best with it, right?"

Blood seemed to enjoy her longshot reasoning. He gestured to the maid.

"Bring several different blends. If the young lady wants to choose the tea for my tea party, then I want to watch." He let a chuckle slip, but he didn't seem to have time to say anything else; he dropped his eyes back to his papers as the maid made her exit.

The Hatter syndicate is young, she thought, a rehash of his earlier words. No wonder he was overloaded. She sat in silence as he worked.

A few minutes later, the maid carried in a tray covered with an assortment of teas. The different cans and bottles were arrayed like the contents of a treasure chest.

"Sorry to keep you waiting~. Which one will you have~?"

Alice poked through the cans. "If you have a preference," she called to Blood, "now's the time to say it."

"I'm just looking forward to what you choose."

Ever since staying in Heart Castle, Alice had been influenced by Vivaldi and Blood's interest in tea. She considered herself something of an expert. But the wide selection that stared up at her from that tray was daunting enough to make her hesitate.

She saw classic Darjeeling, Assam, Uva…along with herb teas and what she guessed were original blends. It took her a while just to go over the brands.

And she was…worried that Diamonds Blood was just as picky as Hearts/Clover Blood. He probably didn't have a lot of tea parties here, based on the wasted condition of his garden, and the fact that good leaves were probably hard to come by with all the strife in the country. She guessed that this high-quality tea was his *personal* collection.

She eventually narrowed her choice to two options. But when she glanced up, Blood's face was still tilted down, his hand quickly scratching out some notes with a pen. He didn't so much as peek at her.

The guy never seemed stressed from all his work, even if he was obviously overloaded. If he knew how much Alice considered his feelings in picking the tea, it might leave a bad taste in his mouth. He was a proud man.

But she did consider him—silently—as she compared the two cans in her hands. She eventually handed one to the maid and returned the other to the tray.

"Could you brew this up, please?"

"This~?" the maid asked, staring at an unopened herbal tea. "Are you sure this is the one you want~?"

"Yeah."

The maid carried out the overflowing tray, Alice's chosen can resting on top. Alice's lips curled into a small smile as she watched the maid leave the room.

Of course the maid would doubt her decision— Alice had chosen a relatively common tea that she could probably buy at a normal store. But Alice had special memories tied up in that brand...so it was important to her.

It's good for a relaxing drink after work, she thought. *The old Blood said it was one of his favorite herbals.*

That Blood had never looked tired, but he'd recommend the tea to *her* when she was exhausted with everything at Heart Castle. *"I'll bet you want something calming,"* he'd say as he brought out two cups.

She smiled, enjoying the bit of nostalgia. But then she frowned, since that hadn't been so long ago that it *warranted* nostalgia.

She wondered what would happen if she mentioned those memories to Blood. He'd probably make a weird face.

"Sorry to keep you waiting~," the maid called as she reappeared, her tray now bearing a teapot and two cups.

Blood finally looked up from his work. His eyes followed the maid's hands as she poured the tea with practiced ease.

The steaming, amber-colored liquid released a refreshing fragrance into the room. The smell alone had a healing effect on Alice.

Blood seemed to feel the same. He stood from his desk and headed for the sofa opposite her.

"Herbal tea?" he asked.

"Yeah. Smells nice, right?"

"I can't say I *dislike* the smell." The maid left the

room as Blood lifted a teacup and inhaled deeply.

Alice picked up her own cup and took a sip. The warm, soothing liquid rolled over her tongue, flashing her back to the last time she'd had it. Her face relaxed unconsciously. "Delicious," she murmured.

"Agreed—it's a favorite of mine among the herbals. I'd used all mine up; a new supply only came in last period."

"Oh yeah?" she asked politely. "I love the smell, and it's so easy to drink."

"Hn."

Blood had requested conversation over the tea, but he seemed to have forgotten that. He just slowly sipped, which made Alice follow suit.

He finally returned both the cup and saucer to the tray. He folded his hands together and fixed his eyes on her.

She didn't sense harassment or hostility in his gaze—but he did seem restless. Like he was searching for something. She waited, but he didn't say anything.

Finally, Alice broke the eye contact. She stood from her sofa.

"I should be getting to work," she murmured. "And you're obviously busy here—"

"How do you know so much about me, young lady?"

The ice in his voice sucked the warmth out of the room.

"H-huh?" Alice blurted. The question was so sudden that she didn't know how to answer.

The man flicked his teacup. The ceramic cup clacked loudly as it jostled on its saucer.

"You acted like we were friends from the very first moment we met," he said darkly. "The first time I called you to this room, you didn't ask anyone for directions. You put all my books exactly where they should be. And now you choose a tea you know I'd like." His eyes narrowed. "These aren't things you could've learned from asking other people about me."

Alice swallowed. She tried a weak laugh.

"You're overthinking this," she offered. "I knew your first name, so I called you that by accident. I heard the location of your room from the maids, and of course I'm good with books considering my day job now. The tea was...a lucky guess."

That clearly wasn't good enough for the head of the Hatter Family. The corners of his mouth curved up as he rose from the sofa.

"If you seriously think I would buy that, then I'm insulted you think so little of me. Coincidence is when something happens *once,* young lady. Three times points to fate. Or do miracles like that happen all the time where you come from?

"After I told you to come to my room, I confirmed with my employees that you never asked for directions. If there's a coincidence that would allow you to traverse this huge mansion in a beeline for my room *without* a single wrong turn, I'd love to hear about it."

"......"

She couldn't answer that one. At the time, she'd figured the head boss wouldn't change rooms on a whim, so she'd just walked to the same room she was used to in Hearts and Clover. That had clearly been a mistake.

"You choosing this tea is the last straw. Not even Elliot knows how much I like it. So let's change the question a bit, young lady." He leaned closer to her. "Were you somehow involved with a *different version* of myself?"

Alice was shocked at how certain he sounded. She could only nod.

And to be honest, she probably *had* underestimated Blood of the Country of Diamonds—she never would've dreamed he'd see through so much. Maybe he seemed younger than the one she'd known, but Blood Dupre was still Blood Dupre.

It's not worth hiding the facts now. She took a breath.

"You're right," she said quietly. "I've met you before—well, I met the Blood Dupre of the Countries of Hearts and Clover."

"You *met* him?" Blood asked softly. "It sounds like you did more than that."

"We were…friends. That's all."

She went on to repeat a lot of what she'd told Jericho in the museum—what the Hatters and the other territories were like in the other countries, and what kind of relationship she had with them. When she was finished, Blood finally crossed his arms and stared down at her.

"So that's how you knew about my private rose garden. A version of me in a different country invited you into it."

"It didn't happen right away…but yeah, he let me in there more than once."

Red roses and green vines; a man in a white suit and a beautiful woman in a red dress. Alice couldn't forget that precious memory if she tried. It was a rose-rimmed world that perfectly suited the brother and sister. Just recalling it seemed to bathe her in the lush fragrance of the flowers.

Blood's voice cut through her thoughts.

"Who else knows that you were involved with me in a different country?"

She paused at that. "I discussed it at the museum with Jericho," she admitted. "If I talked to anyone else about it, they just heard it as random complaints."

Blood puffed out a breath at her answer. "The Gravekeeper?" he muttered. "If your story is true, why did you tell *him* first? You claim you didn't know him before this country."

"It's *because* I've never met him before that he's easier to talk to." She didn't add the mundane point that Jericho's calm demeanor and the odd atmosphere of the museum had all encouraged her to open up to him.

But it seemed that Blood didn't allow for the mundane.

"I see," he said ominously. "It seems that you're good at getting under people's skin, young lady."

Alice's face distorted. "I wasn't trying to get under anyone's *skin,*" she snapped.

"But you did. First that other Blood Dupre, then me, then you moved on to the Gravekeeper. I don't approve of your tastes."

Alice's jaw dropped. "Blood!"

The Mafia boss didn't back off. In fact, his smile only grew colder.

"What's the appeal of a man who's already dead?" he spat. "You're even stranger than I thought you were."

"Will you stop saying that? Jericho is a living, breathing person." She scowled. "And I like to talk to *different people* with *different opinions.* He's not like the Blood I know from other countries. And neither are you."

Maybe Blood didn't believe her; he only glared. Alice was already irritated, but his hostile gaze spoke volumes about how pointless the conversation had become.

"If we're done talking," she said through her teeth, "then I should get back to work." She slapped the table louder than she needed to as she rose to her feet.

She marched to the door without looking back. As she reached for the knob, his voice rang through the room behind her.

"The next Survey Meeting is coming up."

"......"

"If you plan on any more *trysts* with the Gravekeeper, I suggest you keep a low profile. If someone like Elliot saw you, it could turn into a noisy problem."

"Thanks for the warning," she snarled, ripping the door open.

As Alice stomped out of the room, the guards on either side of the door flashed her curious looks. Alice ignored them and stormed down the hallway.

"Blood is such an idiot!" she hissed to herself.

"Why does he always say garbage like that?"

Every recollection of his words put her more and more on edge. It felt like she'd caught that disease from the Red Queen, even though Vivaldi wasn't around to infect her.

Blood of the other countries had always used sexual harassment or provocative words to rile her up. He'd shoot things off in a fake malevolent voice. She couldn't count the number of times he'd used sarcasm to avoid getting to the point.

He'd never irritated her as badly as this. She was a fool for assuming he was a straight talker—she should have answered him with banter.

But if that were true, then why was she suddenly so angry? She didn't know, and that uncertainty frayed her nerves.

She swiftly climbed the steps. When she finally stepped into the reference library, Alice stopped.

"Nn…!"

Her balance wavered as the inside of her head went numb. A sudden dizziness made her knees wobble.

She automatically stuck her hand out to steady

herself. If the wall hadn't been there, she surely would've crumpled to the ground.

She furrowed her brow. "I've felt dizzy like this before," she breathed to herself. "When Blood first threw me in a cell when I got to Diamonds. But it's happened a few other times, too, hasn't it?"

The *intensity* of the dizziness had varied, though. Sometimes she just steadied herself against a table, other times she was ready to faint.

Was she just so mad that her blood pressure had spiked? But with the way she'd left Blood's room, there was *no way* she was going to tell him she couldn't work because she felt sick.

It's just the blood rushing to my head, she told herself. *It'll pass if I just calm down.*

She swallowed bile and shakily got to work.

ACT 5

A Fog of Gun Smoke

Alice cut the binding around a pile of books in the reference library. "That should do it," she called to the maid. "I think this is the last bundle."

"Right~! All the rest go to the incinerator, so if we just throw these in the vault, we should be all set~."

Alice smiled. "Good work."

Alice hadn't expected to get so much exercise in the reference library, but a lot of her job boiled down to manual labor, considering all the books she had to lug around in her organization process. When adding a category, she often had to reshelf the entire collection.

And now she had to archive unneeded research

publications. She tapped a fist on the pile in front of her.

"I've never been to the vault. Where is it? I don't have anything to do after this, so I'll take them."

"Huh~? You'll take them yourself~? You'll spoil me~!"

"This is a small batch. Just tell me where to go."

After the maid gave her directions, Alice clutched the books to her chest and left the library. She passed other mobsters in the hallway, but thankfully, none of them threw her suspicious glances.

She'd expected a worse attitude from everyone after her argument with Blood, but nothing seemed to have changed. Even Elliot and the twins acted normally. If they'd heard that Alice had been friends with their other-country versions, they didn't let on.

Blood probably didn't tell anyone what I said. She didn't know why he hadn't, but even now, when she thought back on their conversation, an unspeakable frustration welled up in her.

The weird dizziness had passed, thankfully. She didn't know if her irritation with Blood or simple exhaustion had caused it, but she figured the various stresses had combined to take their toll on her health.

Still clutching the books, she walked into a section of the outdoor mansion grounds she didn't normally visit. It was even more choked with weeds than the garden. As she walked the overgrown path, a sudden roar made her jump.

Voices—*lots* of voices—rolled through the air from nearby. It sounded like a frenzied mob.

"Huh?!"

She didn't expect fighting, since the Survey Meetings were still going on. But when gunfire suddenly exploded elsewhere, her blood turned to ice.

There had been attacks on the main gate before, but now Alice stood right beside the mansion itself. She'd never heard of an attack this far into the grounds.

She needed a place to hide. She ran for the vault, hoping she'd find something to duck behind there.

When she finally arrived at the vault, she dropped the burden of her books to the ground and tried to catch her breath. She ducked down into the shadow of the vault and tried to keep as still as she could.

A moment later, footsteps crunched on the ground.

"Who could that be?" someone murmured.

She expected it to either be one of the attackers, or someone from the mansion trying to head the enemy off. Alice poked her head out slightly to get a better look.

She was shocked to see that it was Blood. He gripped his gun in one hand, his gait surprisingly casual as his eyes roamed around the area.

Alice had no idea what he was looking for, but decided against calling out. She ducked back into the shadows just as Blood stiffened.

He narrowed his eyes and re-gripped his gun.

"Got you, Hatter! You're *dead!*"

Men from all directions ran into Alice's line of sight, their guns trained on Blood. He was *massively* outgunned.

"......"

Blood didn't say a word. He just whipped up his weapon and fired a volley of bullets in a circle around him, creating a domino effect of falling, screaming men.

Alice smelled the sharp stink of iron and smoke that she'd never gotten used to. By the time the air cleared, the fight was over.

Enemy blood splatters stained Blood's white clothes. Clearly unharmed, he rubbed a red drop from his cheek and dropped his eyes to the gun in his hand.

Alice breathed a sigh of relief. She hadn't said more than a few words to him since their argument, but she still didn't want to see him get *hurt* or anything.

When no more enemies entered the clearing, Blood shifted his gun back into its cane form. Unfortunately, the sound of gunfire in the distance hadn't lessened in the slightest—which meant the attack on the mansion was still underway.

When he started to walk again, Alice stood up from her hiding place in the shadow of the vault.

"Bloo—"

Just as she was about to run after him, she froze.

The barrel of a gun peeked through a hole in a thicket, aimed at Blood's back. Almost uncannily like the first time she'd been shot at in Hatter Mansion.

It's Blood, so he probably noticed? Although…

She flashed back to a moment in Clover—when some troops waiting in ambush tried to attack Blood during the Assembly. Blood hadn't even used his gun—he'd just beaten them off with his cane, complaining that he was bored with "incompetent assassins."

But that Blood, who spat insults at men who had tried to kill him, wasn't the man in the blood-spattered coat who walked away from her now.

Her usual assumption that he'd want her to protect herself flew out of her mind. She was afraid *he didn't see the hidden gun.*

"Blood!" she cried, leaping out of the shadows. "Watch out!"

He whipped towards her, clearly stunned. But then his face darkened as he threw out an arm.

"Do you have a death wish?!" he shouted.

A heavy shot rang out behind her. Something burned across the flesh of her left arm.

"Rrgh!" Rather than change his cane again, Blood tore a gun from his breast pocket and fired past Alice's shoulder. Alice heard a thump and a moan behind her.

Alice dizzily stepped back as Blood ran at her. Her gripped her left arm, which she realized, belatedly, had been *shot.*

He pressed his hand over the blood welling up on her skin. "You're wounded," he said quickly.

"Blood, um…"

"Do me a favor and shut up!"

Alice swallowed, her mind too cloudy to argue.

He was…yelling at her. And clearly frustrated. Her face fell despite her attempts to stop it.

*I think this is the first time Blood's ever **yelled** at me,* she thought dumbly. *The old Blood wasn't the… yelling type.*

And judging from his reaction, he *had* sensed the gunman and was trying to lure him out or something. She suddenly felt very stupid for jumping out into the open and getting herself hurt.

Her shoulders slumped, but he didn't seem to notice.

"Can you move your fingers?" he suddenly asked. "There isn't much blood, but I want to check for nerve damage."

"Uh…" Alice moved her fingers as ordered, then

twisted her face at the stab of resonating pain.

But Blood breathed a sigh of relief. "If it hurts," he said, "that's proof the nerves are still working."

"I-I guess that makes sense…"

As the shock slowly sloughed off her, she felt tears build up in her eyes. She tried to blink them away as the rumble of feet rolled in from nearby.

She turned to see a group of the Hatter mobsters, all dressed in their white suits, run up behind her. Elliot waved his gun at their leader.

"Blood!" he shouted. "Where's the rest of them?!"

"I cleared the area. How did you do?"

"We pushed 'em all out~."

"We gave them a pretty thorough beating~. They won't be back again for a long time~."

"I see." Blood looked from his men, to Alice, back to his men again.

Alice wasn't sure Elliot even noticed her. He nodded at Blood, clearly impressed. "Nice! You offered them an opening and lured them into the mansion so we could take 'em down. I was so fed up with their crap—"

"Elliot, you handle the clean-up. I have other

business." Blood gripped the hand on Alice's good arm. "Come, young lady."

"Huh? But Blood…" Elliot's bursting pride slowly drained from his face.

Alice groaned involuntarily as Blood dragged her to her feet, but she had no time to object or resist. Her mind spun from the throbbing pain in her arm. She lost all track of what he was saying.

Elliot's ears twitched curiously. "Hey, Blood! What's that woman—hggh!"

One blow from Blood's cane sent Elliot crumpling to the ground.

"Out of my way," Blood snapped. "I just told you to clean up. **Do it.**"

Blood pulled Alice past his fallen second-in-command and back toward the mansion. Once inside, Alice was surprised to see them headed for *his* room. She stumbled behind him.

He finally dragged her to his sofas and released her. "Sit down," he ordered.

"No, um…"

"Young lady?" In response, Blood mimed how he'd just beaten Elliot with his cane.

Alice shrank back from the threat and dropped onto the sofa. "I-if you insist."

Blood fetched a small box from somewhere. His face tight with annoyance, he tossed aside his jacket and hat and sat next to her.

"Wh-what are you doing?"

"First aid. What does it look like?"

He flipped open the box. Alice's eyes fell on a white bandage and a small bottle filled with medicine.

"R-right," she breathed. "Then you'll just patch me up?"

He tugged off his gloves. And then Blood Dupre, head of the Hatter Family, feared Mafia boss of the Country of Diamonds, gently applied first aid to the Outsider on his couch.

Alice stared fixedly at his profile, not sure this was really happening. He leaned over her wound as he cleaned it. His blue-green eyes locked on his work as a bothered sigh leaked from his lips.

Oh my God.

"...You look like you want to say something," he said thinly.

Alice swallowed. "I just…didn't expect you to do something like this for me. Don't you think helping other people is pointless?"

Confronted by the same words he'd used when Alice had saved his maid, Blood's mouth snapped shut.

Alice had jumped out from her hiding place of her own free will. It wasn't Blood's fault she was shot. And considering what Elliot had said, she'd *gotten in the way* of some plan that had been doing fine without her.

But Blood didn't answer Alice's comment. He didn't even seem annoyed that she'd blundered into his plan. He just softly ran his bare fingers over Alice's blood-smeared arm.

"I need to use the disinfectant," he murmured. "This will sting a little."

"Okay… Ow!"

Alice clenched her teeth, swallowing a hiss as her injury burned. Blood reduced his pressure on the wound.

After washing the dirt and blood away, he wiped her down with clean gauze. Maybe it was because he was good at this, or because he'd lightened his touch, but the pain started to drain away.

"……"

The atmosphere around them felt very different from the last time she'd been in the room. She couldn't describe it. Things felt…a little awkward.

Her eyes fell to his fingers, normally hidden under his gloves. They were long and slender, but angular. Masculine.

How can his fingers look that good when he's wiping up blood?

He finally finished securing the gauze. He paused.

"In the other countries, did you…"

Alice's eyes snapped up at his sudden murmur. "Huh?"

He didn't meet her gaze. Only his lips moved.

"I just wondered if you did something similar for the Blood Dupre of the other countries. You know—recklessly jumping in front of a gun."

Alice winced. "No way—I'm no hero. I got caught up in dangerous situations because of him, sure, but I never jumped into the line of fire or anything."

He let a breath out through his nose. "I thought as much. Something like that would be suicidal. And I doubt the me of the other countries would be so fond of an idiot." A mysterious, confused look filled his eyes as he dragged his gaze around Alice's face.

"Then…why did you try to protect me?" he asked at last. "You did the same thing for my maid the first time we met. You're irreplaceable. Risking yourself for us is pointless."

Alice sighed. "God, I've heard that argument so many times in this world. Even the 'you' of the other countries said it to me. You're replaceable, *you're replaceable*."

She threw up her good hand. "I don't care. You and your maid are both living people, so protecting you isn't pointless to *me*."

"It *is* pointless," Blood insisted. "Someone can replace her and even me, and *nothing* will change. Your view is only warped because there's no replacement to take *your* place."

Maybe Blood meant to make the statement brutal, like when Alice had protected the maid…but his voice came out much softer than expected.

He gave the bandage one more tug. Alice couldn't figure out his thoughts as he brought his face closer to the gauze.

He brushed his lips over it.

Alice froze. She stared at him, shocked, as he looked up from her wound and flashed a knowing smile.

"B-Blood," she breathed.

"I assume *that's* something the Blood Dupre of the other countries wouldn't do. Thank you, Alice."

"......"

*Did he…just call me by my name? While **thanking** me?!*

Maybe the actions didn't mean that much on their own, but together… It seemed like he was finally getting a little closer to her. Feeling welled up in her and spread a smile across her face.

He raised an eyebrow. "You're wounded. What are you smiling for? Unless you *like* pain…"

"No!" she blurted back. "I hate things that hurt! I just thought that…this situation didn't end up *all* bad."

"You're a strange young lady."

Alice met Blood's dubious words with a smile as she stood from the sofa. Her arm throbbed slightly, but nothing bad enough to concern her.

"I should thank you for the first aid," she said. "So, well…thank you. Do you mind if I go back to my room now?"

Blood was a busy man, so she figured she'd leave while she was ahead. But as she walked back to the door, he called out to her.

"Wait. There's one thing I want to say first."

Alice turned. He stood in front of the sofa, the medicine box still clutched in his hand.

"Yeah?"

"You're on leave from your job while that heals."

Alice blinked. "Huh? It's not bad enough to get in the way of—"

"Your wound won't just heal in the next time period—not yet, anyway. Don't tax yourself."

"……"

"Well? Will you take the leave?"

Phrasing it as a question rather than an order was probably him trying to be considerate. She softened.

It's weird seeing him so open and honest, she

thought. *But that's nice every once in a while.*

"Thank you," she answered at last. "I'll take you up on that."

"Mm. You should take me up while there's still something to take."

Alice couldn't argue with that. She nodded…

A smile floated across Blood's lips.

Alice assumed she'd have a lot of time on her hands while on leave from her job—it was the only thing she *did* with her days. But before she could get anxious over the impending restlessness, Blood came to her. He visited her guest room the very next time period after her injury.

He carried a stack of books in his arms, his medicine box balanced on top of them. "You seem *guilty* about taking time off from your job," he commented as he swept into her room. "So here."

Her eyes widened. She turned from her place by the window.

"Did you…bring those books for me?"

"No, I enjoy carting them around for no reason," he drawled. "How's the arm?"

Alice quickly walked over to a chair. Unlike Blood's quarters, her room didn't have couches— just a few scattered chairs. But when she tried to carry one over, Blood caught her by the shoulder.

"Just sit down," he told her, pushing her into the chair herself. "The injured shouldn't wander around *carrying* things."

He dropped the books onto a nearby desk, then dragged a chair closer to hers. He gripped her wounded arm as he sat down.

Did he intend to change the bandage himself? He looked so serious…and he hadn't brought a maid.

She figured his initial treatment was just an urgency thing, but now there was no blood dripping down her arm. For a man that busy to come to her room for a routine check-up… She was a little baffled, honestly.

Maybe her question showed in her face, because Blood's eyebrows knit together.

"What?"

She squirmed a little. "Uh…a wound like this is nothing to you people, right? Did you come all the way here to…check on my health?"

She'd *wanted* to ask if he was worried about her, but in her panic, the words came out differently. And she didn't want to seem…conceited.

"True," Blood answered as he unwound her bandage. "*We* wouldn't worry about something like this. But you have no replacement, and you were hurt protecting me."

"You didn't *need* my protection, though. I actually gummed up your plan."

Blood gave a low chuckle. "Then consider it chivalry," he answered, "for a man to take responsibility at a time like this."

She grimaced. "I'm not stupid enough to expect chivalry from a *Mob boss*."

"I'm hurt you think so little of me. I may be Mafia, but I have a sense of responsibility, thank you. When a powerless woman takes a bullet meant for me, I feel bad."

He carefully laid a medicinal gauze pad over the wound. Alice felt a chill leak from it through her skin, down to the bone. But unlike last time, it didn't hurt.

His hands were just as gentle.

"I should probably tell you," she said as he worked, "I didn't try to protect you because you're my landlord right now. I just...didn't want to stand there and watch you get hurt."

"I know. And I'm not trying to repay you as your host or as someone who owes you his life." He glanced up. "I'm doing this because I *want* to. So give me that, at least."

Alice finally closed her mouth. "Okay," she mumbled.

She had to admit, she really enjoyed the new comfort she felt around him. Sitting in that room as he bandaged her arm felt...relaxed. Like how she and the old Blood would get together just to read in silence.

The memory dragged her eyes to the pile of books. "So...what did you bring me?" she asked.

"Mystery novels and some travelogues. When you've gone through them, I can send more, but the next Survey Meeting will probably be starting by then." His forehead creased, and frustration twisted his mouth into a wry smile. "Ah, the Survey Meeting. Dammit—I'd blissfully forgotten about it for a moment."

Alice tried not to smile. "I wonder what will come first," she mused aloud. "The meeting, or my wound healing up?"

Alice had never really figured out the flow of time in Wonderland. The random occurrences of daytime, evening, or night didn't even last the same length of time. The periods could end quickly or stretch forever.

But Blood seemed to interpret her comment very differently. "I hope you don't need to attend with a scar," he drawled. "Always a shame to see that on a lady's smooth skin. At the very least, I'd like a scar with a more pleasing...shape."

He drew his lips near her arm again, almost a tease, and low-level panic twisted her stomach. She tightened.

"Stop it," she blurted.

Blood shot her a dissatisfied look, then sat up straight to face her.

"Don't be shy," he drawled. "You were on intimate terms with the *other* Blood Dupre."

"I told you, our relationship...wasn't like that."

He didn't reply. Those blue-green eyes bore into her.

Another tremor went through her body, like it had when he'd moved to kiss her arm again. It wasn't fear...it was some other feeling she couldn't pinpoint.

Alice started to speak quickly, her words almost a babble.

"Besides, you're not...the same guy as that Blood. You're not as nonchalant as he was, and you seem like you're in more danger..."

She'd always felt a languid self-possession in the other Blood, along with something else she couldn't define. A certain...humanity?

Blood's face clouded over slightly. "Are you saying I can't *handle* myself?"

"Maybe a little? Ugh, how can I put this..." Alice averted her eyes. "I know you're really independent, but there's something that makes me worry about you. Makes me want to help *you*. At least, right now."

"......"

Blood suddenly stood, the medicine box tucked under his arm. He let out a breath.

"I'm done with the bandage," he said evenly. "I hope it's healed by the Survey Meeting. What a pain."

Alice frowned, a little uncomfortable with his sudden shift in attitude. "I guess that's true," she agreed. "And it'll probably be ugly, too."

Maybe I insulted him. She watched him turn his back on her and march for the door.

Elliot nearly crashed into him as he burst into the room.

"Blood! Sorry to bother you, but I needed to check something with..." Elliot's face darkened as he noticed Alice. "What the hell are *you* doing here?"

Alice bristled. "This guest room was assigned to me," she snapped. *Don't take your problems out on me,* she added silently.

"It doesn't concern you," Blood said in the same flat tone. "We have work. Move it, Elliot."

Looking perturbed, Elliot left the room so Blood could follow.

"Blood...?" she called.

He didn't turn back. The door slammed shut behind him.

"Big Sis, Big Sis! Wanna come gamblin' with us? This time we're sure to win a jackpot!"

"Last time, we couldn't make any money 'cause we got burned by the fees. So this time, we'd better cash in!"

Alice flashed a sardonic grin at the twins crowding around her. They'd waited until the group had entered Diamond Castle for the Survey Meeting, but literally not a second longer.

In the other countries, she would've lectured them for gambling while underage. But they only took adult form here, so she knew they wouldn't listen. While formulating a *new* argument against them betting all their hard-earned pay, she felt a sharp look burning into her side.

"......"

She sighed. "Elliot," she muttered, "I'm not planning to run off. I hear anyone can bet on the

Survey Meeting, but if you hate it that much, I won't even try."

"Like I'd believe *anything* coming out of your mouth when you hang out with the Gravekeeper," Elliot spat. "Right, Blood?"

"I wonder," Blood said sharply, cutting off Elliot's words.

Alice fiddled with her bandage. Blood's timely treatments had helped, and she was definitely on the mend…but the closeness between them had vanished, and he was in a rotten mood. She'd never seen him so *obvious* about it.

What got him so upset? she thought tiredly. She wanted to ask, but Blood always seemed to have Elliot by his side; she couldn't find any decent openings to cut in.

She felt like she was back at square one with Blood—not even close enough to be friends. Had she imagined that intimacy when she'd been hurt? He'd definitely acted like more than a landlord.

"Thank you, Alice."

He'd kissed her wound. And that, along with his heartfelt, respectful words had crossed some sort of border. Now that felt like a *new* wound. A sigh leaked through her lips.

"...I feel a little lonely."

Alice didn't realize she'd said it out loud until the twins jumped on her.

"What'd you say?" Dee chirped. "Your wallet's lonely for some money?"

Dum beamed. "Then let's all fill the voids together!"

She tried to brush off the slip. "It's not that," she said quickly. "Just talking to myself." She let her eyes wander to the gambling ticket windows.

Once she'd started worrying about Blood, she'd begun to *expect* things from him. The closer she got to him, the more she wanted to understand him. But she knew that things couldn't happen too fast or one of them would be left scrambling.

She frowned. Jericho had been kind and respectful from the second she'd met him. What would her life be like if he'd been the *first* person she ran into in Diamonds...?

She mulled over the thought as she placed a paltry bet at the window. When she returned to the group, only Elliot stood there. The twins were grilling a tipster at another window, and Blood had vanished.

"Oh." She looked around. "Elliot, where's Blood?"

"He had *business,*" he muttered. "He's a busy guy."

Unlike me? Alice thought as Elliot glowered.

"I know that," she answered sourly. "Thanks."

Elliot turned from her to fly off the handle at the twins. "Will you two just make up your minds?!" he yelled. "If you're not here when we need to go, we're leaving your asses behind!"

Dee flicked his head from the ticket window to make a face. "Shut up, ya dumb rabbit! We're tryin' to concentrate."

"The meetin' can go a bunch of different ways," Dum added. "It's not easy to pick! If you screw up our thinkin', you gotta pay for our losses!"

Elliot growled. "You little…! You two need to be taken down a peg!" He stormed toward them, but not before glancing back at Alice.

"Listen!" he barked. "You take *one step* from this area while I'm not here, and you're gonna get it!"

Alice jumped a little at the intensity. "R-right," she blurted.

She wiped her sweaty palms on her dress and tried to entertain herself. The people-watching was pretty good—the Survey Meeting, its gambling ring, and the Garden Party were a country-wide event. Most of the Diamonds citizens had focused around the ticket windows, crowding around to place their bets. As she watched the eager crowds, a finger tapped her shoulder.

"Yo. It's been a while, Alice."

She turned to the familiar voice. Jericho, back in his glasses and black suit, grinned down at her.

"Jericho." She smiled. "Thank you so much for before."

Alice paused to check that Elliot wasn't watching. Sure enough, he was still arguing with the twins— which was probably why Jericho had popped over.

Jericho followed her gaze and flashed a sarcastic smile. "As always, you're right in the middle of the loudest screams." His eyes dropped to her bandage. "Hm? What happened to your arm?"

"Oh, this? It's almost completely healed now. It still looks pretty gross, but it doesn't hurt anymore."

His face softened in sympathy. "Did someone in

the Hatter clan do that?"

"Nah. Just got hit by a stray bullet."

"I guess a Mafia turf war is tough for an amateur."

She shrugged. "True. And this is definitely not an easy world for an Outsider like me."

She'd seen bullets and blood plenty of times in Wonderland. But she hadn't gotten used to it. She didn't *want* to.

Her face fell as her mind wandered back to her injury. She was still confused about Blood treating her…and the kiss. *The kiss.* She couldn't figure out the meaning behind his touch. She felt emotions she wanted to pursue tangled up with feelings she'd rather leave alone.

She still had no answer. She sighed and waved a hand, eager to focus on anything else.

"You came all the way to my territory for my advice before," Jericho mumbled, "but it seems to have backfired, hm? You tried to turn the tables, and this was the result."

Alice blinked. "What? No, not at all! Don't worry about it. Besides." She chuckled weakly. "That wasn't really what I would call 'advice.'"

Jericho smiled at that.

He seems like such a stable guy, she thought.

"At the very least," he offered, "you've made a place for yourself at the Hatters'. You should take pride in that."

He suddenly slapped her on the shoulder with strength she didn't expect. She cried out and stumbled, and in a rush, Jericho held out a steadying hand.

"Sorry! I didn't mean to do that so hard... Are you suffering from something *other* than the gunshot?"

Alice swallowed. "No, I'm fine. But I guess I've had a few dizzy spells lately. I'll have to be careful about that..."

The dizziness that crept up on Alice unawares. She'd started to worry about it, even if she had no other symptoms. She wondered if it was time for her to go to a hospital... A vague dread settled in her stomach.

*I always give Nightmare a hard time when **he** doesn't go,* she thought. It felt weird to be on the other side of that advice for once.

Jericho's features abruptly drew together in

concern. "Dizziness?" he repeated.

"Yeah," she answered with a light laugh. "It happens all of a sudden, and it's hard to breathe. I don't know the reason, but—huh?"

Jericho suddenly reached out and touched the muscles of her neck. The hard tips of his fingers twitched over her skin.

"J-Jericho?" Alice stared up at him in surprise.

Realization lit up his own face. He abruptly dropped his hand.

"Uh, sorry," he said quickly. "I should've...asked, at least, before touching you."

"Yeah, but...okay. Why did you do that?"

He looked away. "I wanted to check your pulse," he murmured. "And that's the quickest way to find it. Sorry to scare you like that."

She frowned. "It's not a big deal, you just... surprised me. I'm fine, Jericho."

Jericho's closed, apologetic expression melted away. He stared down at her in fascination.

His eyes softened, like he was gazing at an old memory. Alice sensed sadness behind it.

"Good. That eases my mind. I'll...see you later."

The Gravekeeper spun on his heel and walked away. He disappeared into the crowd just as Alice realized why he'd left so fast.

Blood appeared beside her.

"The Gravekeeper," he said darkly. "I knew it."

Alice cringed slightly. "Blood! When did you get back?"

"A moment ago." He snorted. "Maybe you didn't notice because you were drowning in pleasure."

Alice scowled. After his vanishing act and abrupt return, she didn't like him immediately needling her.

"Knock it off, Blood."

He turned exasperated eyes on her. He suddenly shoved a vial with a drug label into her hands.

"What's this?" she asked.

"Medicine."

"Well, I can see *that!* What *kind* of medicine?" She squinted at the label.

And stopped.

Amidst the directions and precautions, she saw the words "to reduce scarring."

It only took a time period for wounds to vanish on people in Wonderland—and that included scars.

Why did this medicine even exist here? Blood certainly didn't need it.

She looked fearfully back at him. Trepidation crept up her spine.

"You didn't...leave to buy this, did you?" she croaked.

Blood answered with a shrug. "I didn't think you'd be taking that time to flirt with the Gravekeeper."

She glared at him. "I wasn't flirting."

He returned the look, danger looming behind his eyes.

"You're pretty cold to me as I am now," he said in a low voice. "I'll bet you weren't like this with the *other* Blood Dupre."

"What's that supposed to mean?"

"You heard me. If you're going to show a pretty face to men outside the territory, you could at least make your landlord happy, too."

"Happy...?" Her hand clenched over the vial. "I've told you a million times—I'm just being *civil* with Jericho. I barely know him—we're not even close enough to be *friends!*"

She stopped as his gloved fingers suddenly brushed the pulse at her neck.

She jerked back, trembling. "Wh-what was that for?!"

He grunted. "You didn't look that shocked when the Gravekeeper touched you." His lips curved in a dark smile. "Unless you consider me more of a sexual threat."

Alice finally lost her patience. She roughly knocked his arm away.

"Jericho surprised me, so I was too shocked to react! It was just a *normal reaction* to someone surprising me. The only kind of person who *wouldn't* react would either be numb below the eyebrows or have nerves of steel. God, get over yourself!"

"......"

Blood glowered at her. She glowered back.

The twins suddenly ran up, breaking the tension. With screams.

"Boss!" Dee cried. "I think we made a perfect bet this time! But ya can't win today, okay? Ya gotta pull your punches for our plan to work."

"Yeah!" Dum shouted. "Even if you try to win, ya

can't do it by much. Just do it right, okay?"

Alice sighed at the same moment Blood did.

Elliot walked up behind the twins, a betting voucher proudly clutched in his hand. It looked like the twins had even convinced *him* to gamble.

"Are you brats stupid?" he barked. "I put a marker on Blood for the win! It's only natural, right, Blood?"

"I'm done with all of this." Blood sucked his teeth and whacked Elliot across the face with his cane. As Elliot grunted and rubbed his cheek, Blood strode past him. The twins ran to follow, gesturing for Alice to come along.

"So who'd ya finally bet on, Big Sis?"

"We can use it on our next bet, so tell us!"

Alice winced at their screeches. "Well…this is the first time I've ever placed a bet, so I just bet on us."

"But what *rank* did you put us? That's the important part!"

"Yeah, tell us!"

Her bad feelings started to melt away. With a wry smile, she flicked up her index finger.

"You'll just have to wait until it's over to find out. For now, it's a secret."

"Wha?!" Dee threw up his arms. "Big Sis, now you're just bein' mean!"

"Boo! Everybody's gotta profit or it's no fair!"

"Yeah, yeah."

With dry laughter, Alice dodged every one of the twins' questions. They danced around her and wheedled even as they entered the Survey Meeting's arena.

The game hadn't changed since Round One— along with the numbers proclaiming the size of each territory, the leaders could strategize and add in the force that they chose. Blood took his position and made his moves without speaking.

But the Gravekeeper won the day, with the Castle in second place. Hatter Mansion was third, above only the Station.

The shift in winners helped bring the arena to a thundering climax.

Alice leaned back in her seat. She couldn't figure out what force Blood had chosen to use...and neither could Elliot, apparently, based on the way his big frame shook.

"It can't be true!" he cried. "This is Blood we're

taking about here! Why aren't you on top, Blood?!"

Blood sneered over his shoulder. "Pipe down," he snapped as he lowered himself into the chair at the front. "You're close enough for the cane, if you want me to *make* you."

Elliot clenched his fists. "I can't take this!"

"*Shut up,* Elliot!"

"Gah!"

The cane whipped behind Blood, cracking into Elliot's orange head. Elliot curled up and groaned in pain.

Alice licked her lips and double-checked the voucher in her hand.

"I don't believe it," she murmured to herself. "I got it right!"

A winning ticket on her very first bet. She hadn't wagered much money, but she was still pleased. The twins leaned over her and pouted in unison.

"Aw... Big Sis got the only win? I had you at second, Boss! What're you gonna do about it?!"

"Me, too! Agh! We shoulda followed her beginner's luck! Now we're gonna make even less than last time!"

Seeing the twins depressed and Elliot hunched over in dejection, Alice couldn't get that excited about her win. Not if she was the only success story among all the Hatter elites.

Blood turned in his chair, his blue-green eyes leveling on her. "Well," he said. "You won. Who would've thought?"

Alice got the feeling he wanted to say something else, but he didn't. She curled her fingers over the ticket.

"I didn't really care if I won. Maybe that's why I *did*."

"Didn't care?" he repeated sourly. "Are you lacking in *desire?* I could never live like that." His eyes burned. "Desire fuels *everything*."

"And greed can eat you alive," she countered. "What I've got is just right for me."

He turned back to the arena.

Alice let out a breath and looked away. The cheers of the crowd filled her ears as the second Survey Meeting came to an end.

ACT 6

Thinking of That Faraway Place

A lice dragged her finger along the row of book spines, shaking her head in regret.

"They're all disorganized again," she sighed.

With her arm healed, she was back at work, only to find how much of her *earlier* work had been undone. She didn't know if her assistant maid had done *anything* in Alice's absence. There was a good chance she hadn't—*everyone* in Hatter Mansion seemed to be incredibly busy in the Country of Diamonds.

Oh, well. Alice turned to the overflowing returns cart and the mountains of piled books. At least the job never got boring.

She pulled unrelated books from the shelf, found the books that *actually* belonged there, and re-shelved the proper tomes. She enjoyed watching the mountains of books shrink as she worked. It felt like giving something a good cleaning.

Especially since dirty clothes and stains just clean themselves in Wonderland. She liked the rare feeling of accomplishment.

As Alice tried to return a book on agriculture to its proper shelf, she noticed a different book mixed in with the others…and without thinking, her hand stopped.

She remembered that title.

"Didn't I last see this in Blood's room?"

She'd personally returned the book to him before. As she pulled the tome out, she slid the agriculture book into its space.

There was no place in the library for the book she now held in her hand. And since she knew where it was supposed to go, she couldn't just leave it.

She frowned.

She'd been…avoiding Blood since that second Survey Meeting—or to be more accurate, ever since he came to treat her wound the second time. She'd gotten fed up with Blood's constant sarcasm, and she had no idea how insufferable he'd get if they were *alone*. She wanted to keep her distance.

...But this is part of my job.

She still had the books Blood had loaned her piled up in her room. She could return them *and* this one.

So she finished her shift, returned to her room, and gathered up all his loaned books. She balanced the new book on top and carried the pile to his room.

The guards stopped her. When she explained why she was there, they exchanged looks.

"We haven't...heard anything about this from the Boss~."

"I know," she replied. "I'm not here because Blood asked me this time. I'm just...returning some books mixed into the reference collection."

They didn't seem convinced. One of them rapped on the door.

"Boss, the young miss is here~. Will you see her~?"

"Did she have an appointment?" Even muffled by the door, his voice still had that recent, irritated edge to it.

"No. She says she's here to return books~."

For a second Alice hoped he wouldn't let her in—then she could give the books to the guards and be done with it. But the door suddenly swung open.

"Uh… Hi, Blood."

"Returning books? Fine. Come in."

He seemed prickly, but he widened the door. As she followed him into the room, the guards shut the door behind her.

"Do you want me to return them to your shelves?"

"You're the librarian," he replied calmly. "So yes."

She watched him head for a sofa rather than his desk. Was he taking a break? As he lowered himself onto the plush, she headed for Blood's bookshelves.

She'd only slid a few tomes into their proper places when he called to her.

"Alice."

She swallowed. "What?" she asked, her voice a little weak. She tried to stay calm as she slowly turned.

He loomed right behind her. She hadn't heard a single footstep.

For a second, she was oddly impressed by the stealth of a Mafia boss. He tilted his head down at her.

"…What was the other Blood Dupre to you?" he asked in a low rumble.

There was a short pause before he asked. Alice figured that the question had some extra significance to Blood, but she answered as she always did.

"We were friends. End of story."

"I can't tell if you're a good liar or not." His eyes narrowed. "If you were just *friends,* my touch at the Survey Meeting wouldn't have made you jump."

"I've told you *so many times,* Blood. You're imagining things!"

"Am I?"

Blood suddenly surged forward, making Alice slap her back against the bookshelf. He stretched his arms out on either side of her, resting his gloved hands on the tomes…and effectively trapping her.

"No matter how the world turns," he murmured, "I'm still myself. And I don't think I'd just sit there with a fascinating young woman like you close by."

His blue-green eyes dragged all over her body, sending a shiver down her spine.

Alice quickly shook her head. "Nothing happened," she insisted. "It was *friendship.*"

The other Blood had never cornered her like this. To him, Alice was just a rare Outsider visiting from a different territory. He gave her treatises on tea and books to borrow, when Elliot wasn't also shoving carrot cuisine into her face. She knew that it was a real accomplishment to get accepted into the private rose garden of a careful Mafia boss. It made her happy. And, well…proud.

But that Blood had never pressured her into an especially intimate relationship. They shared similar interests and a twisted sense of humor, so they enjoyed each other's company. He was neither too close nor too distant. A perfect range for a close friend.

"Alice…"

She snapped out of her reverie.

"When I'm right in front of you," he said darkly, "don't go daydreaming about another man, even if that man is *me*."

She scowled. "Are you trying to control my *thoughts* now? Don't be ridiculous!"

And seeing Blood here, even Diamonds Blood, ensured that she'd remember those times. She couldn't *not* remember when she stared into those familiar eyes.

His left arm suddenly shifted. He gripped her chin.

And lowered his face toward hers.

Alice panicked. "W-wait!" she blurted as she tried to twist away. "Blood, don't!"

He stopped. She could feel his breath on her mouth. "Why?"

"I-isn't it obvious?!" she stuttered. They weren't even *friends* yet. He couldn't just…kiss her!

Blood's fingers tightened around her chin as he leaned closer.

"No," he rumbled. "It *isn't* obvious! If you're saving yourself for the 'me' of some other country, then just come out and say it." His mouth slanted. "Not that that would stop me."

"I'm not saying that! It's just…the other you never tried this."

Alice swallowed. And she'd never wanted him to. She'd never thought of the old Blood that way.

In response to her words, Blood of the Country of Diamonds furrowed his brow in distaste. He looked like he didn't understand.

"He never tried to kiss you? Even when you were close enough to touch?" He scoffed. "Or did he treat you like something precious, and *that's* why you were obsessed with him?"

"I wasn't obsessed. He was just important to me as a..." The word "friend" died on her lips as he flashed a mocking smile.

"You stopped. So you're finally willing to admit that he was your lover."

"Oh my *God*." Suddenly frustrated beyond belief, Alice slapped his hand away. The look on his face didn't change.

She started to tremble. "Quit talking like that!" she cried. "And you aren't the Blood I know, so don't get any ideas!"

His mouth became a thin line. "He must have been frustrated, having someone so close whom he couldn't touch, couldn't hurt. You say I'm not the same man—and if you're telling the truth, then I agree. I would never have made that choice." He looked away. "If that's the way it was, I can only pity the man."

"Blood…"

He turned from her in disinterest and walked back to his desk. She stared at his gait and that long, familiar back.

He looked so much like the man she knew, but… she was so out of sync with *this* man.

It depressed her.

"You make people do things that aren't in their nature," he said as he lowered himself into his chair. "That may be the proof of your greatest charms, Alice." He leaned back in the seat. "I think that's what makes you Outsiders dangerous."

I can't take this. The longer she stayed, the more he'd twist her words. She crammed the last book into the shelf.

"I've had enough," she said icily. "I'm finished shelving the books, so I'm leaving."

She didn't try to hide her irritation as she double-timed it out of his room. Blood made no attempt to stop her.

That just annoyed her *worse*. She quickened her pace.

Why was he doing this? Why was *this* Blood so

damn critical of her? And…

And was there something wrong with her, too? When he'd gripped her chin and leaned in, had he noticed that her reaction was a moment late?

She hadn't been disgusted by his attempt to kiss her. Knowing that confused her all the more.

It was just Blood making fun of her again, right? She didn't think he was serious about kissing her. It was probably just a capricious impulse for him.

But…when he'd taken her chin in his hand, she'd felt a small heat build up in her. Alice shook her head angrily; she couldn't read too much into something done on a whim.

He thinks I'm in love with the old Blood—and I'm not. I shouldn't have let that get to me.

She'd been so *irritated* to hear him reject her assertions like that. He wouldn't listen.

He was driving her mad.

"Come on, Mom! Forget that picture already!"

"It's much more fun to take your time, sweetie."

In the next gallery over, children were pointing at the museum's various exhibits. Alice saw a woman flash a pained smile at a boy holding her hand.

He tugged at the woman. "But I'm *bored* of that picture—the ones back there look a lot better! We're finally inside the art museum, so let's see the best ones!"

The woman sighed. "What am I going to do with you…?"

Alice's gaze followed the mother and child, and then strayed off down a long hallway. *What's down there?* she wondered. *This place is **big**.*

She hummed, enjoying the anonymity of wandering the art museum alone. She'd slipped out of Hatter Mansion during a mundane work shift, only telling her assistant maid that she was "going out." That was technically following Blood's orders that she not leave without permission, right? The maid would pass it on? And Alice's feet had just led her back to Jericho's territory.

"Mommy, a bunny! And over there! Here's one, too!"

"Don't run—you'll trip and fall!"

Alice watched a rabbit jump out of a picture, then a little girl ran after it. Another rabbit—a white one—bounded over to Alice.

Alice knew it was probably out of the painting, but when she touched it, it felt soft and furry.

That...doesn't feel like a painting.

She didn't have time to be surprised as a shadow fell over her. She looked up into a familiar face.

"It *is* you." Jericho tilted his head. "If you're coming to visit, you should tell the staff."

"Jericho, you're working in the museum today?"

When Alice took her hand from the rabbit and stood again, the creature zipped to a corner of the room unusually fast. She turned from it to face Jericho.

"I didn't expect to catch the busy museum curator just by showing up."

He laughed. "Eh, I'm not good at sitting still—I changed the exhibits a little. Why don't I give you a tour?"

Alice hadn't come to the museum with any goal in mind—she'd just needed some time away from Blood constantly irritating her. A tour sounded like a nice distraction.

"Thanks," she replied.

She followed Jericho down the hallway, and eventually into a room where a *huge* picture of greenery stretched before her. A lot of the exhibits had landscape paintings, but this one was on an entirely different scale.

Someone had painted a forest with sunlight streaming through the leaves on nearly an entire wall. The scene looked as if they had torn down the wall, and on the other side, a real forest stretched out.

Some people were sleeping under the trees, others sat on benches and chatted. Kids clambered up the trees as birds sang overhead.

Alice hummed under her breath. "I like it."

"The theme of this exhibit is 'healing,'" he explained. "And it's titled *Forest*...which is maybe a little too on the nose, heh. There are rivers in the painting and a lake way in the back." He gestured with his head. "You can step into the painting and take a break, if you want."

She flashed him an apologetic smile. "Ah, no.

I'm fine." It was nice of him to offer, but she didn't feel like it.

He smiled back. "Sure. But if you need a break, don't overextend yourself. Just tell me."

For a few moments, she just stared into the tranquil forest. Then she turned her gaze up to him.

"Jericho…"

His eyes widened at the look on her face. "What is it?"

"Um…are you really from this world?" she asked quietly. "Even if I'm an Outsider, you're being so nice to me. It feels too…*normal*."

She was used to *every* leader approaching her "just to see the Outsider." The very few exceptions were the eccentrics or the bigots who wanted to close off Wonderland.

But from the very first moment that she'd met Jericho, he'd treated her like a human being.

Jericho shook his head. "I don't know about 'nice,'" he replied softly. "And I do more dirty work than you think I do."

Alice wondered if he was talking about his work as a Mafia boss. Or the face he wore as the

Gravekeeper, or working as the museum curator…
Even Gowland, who ran the amusement park in
Hearts, had been a leader involved in territory
disputes. She was sure dark acts happened away
from her eyes.

She sighed. "That may be true, but I still think
you're a nice person, Jericho."

"You're free to think what you want. But the
extent of my time's already been decided, so maybe
that's made me philosophical… No, that isn't it."
His eyes lowered to his hand.

He clenched it and nodded to himself.

"One climbs up only to fall," he said. "And if you
think of it that way, the correct path is just resigning
yourself to it. I'm simply awaiting my true end."

Alice furrowed her brow. "The extent of
your time's been decided?" she repeated. She
remembered that she knew next to nothing about
this man.

The man who was already dead. Everyone
always mentioned *death* around him. It was weird
for Wonderland.

As Alice wondered whether to pry further,

Jericho's gaze focused on something past her head. He sucked his teeth.

"Great. Of all times…"

"Wh-what is it?"

A flustered man suddenly ran up, his hands gesturing wildly. "Mr. Curator!" he cried. "We have a problem!"

"Calm down," Jericho ordered. "An attack, right? Tell me the enemy, the location, and any damage done."

"It's definitely the Mad Hatter, but we don't know any more than that. No major damage other than a fence…but they're in the *graveyard,* sir!"

"Fine. I'll be there soon."

Alice didn't have time to interrupt before the man ran off. She flicked wide eyes up at Jericho.

His jaw tightened. "You heard the man. I'm afraid the tour ends here."

"Don't worry about me, but…is this place safe?" Alice looked around at the crowded room. "Should you evacuate the museum?"

He shook his head. "The graveyard is pretty far from here. So for the time being, I consider the inside of this place safe."

"I hope you're right…" Alice wiped her sweaty palms on her skirt.

She suddenly felt nervous in the crowd. A lot of the citizens in that territory probably knew that she lived at Hatter Mansion… Would they think she *led* the Hatters to attack? Just as she was trying to figure out a way to distance herself from the place, Jericho took her hand.

"You need to get away. I'll show you a shortcut."

He led Alice to a space in front of one of the paintings—a busy street scene. The people walking down the street and mingling inside the painting moved as if alive.

"This is the shortcut?" she blurted.

"Yeah. Just do this…and enter the picture."

He stuck his arm straight out and pushed it inside the living painting. Then he gripped her shoulder and shoved her toward it; she lost her balance and gripped the frame to stay on her feet.

"Listen," he said quickly from behind her. "Go in and turn right at the big street. Go straight until a T-intersection, then go left. If you run straight on after that, you'll come out in an area close to the Hatters' territory—but whatever you do, don't go in the other direction! It comes out in a totally different place."

"J-Jericho!" When she righted herself and glanced back, he was already gone. She bit her lip and turned back to the painting.

Half doubting him, she tentatively reached toward the picture as he had done. Her fingers slowly sank into the painting.

"Whoa," she breathed. "This feels weird!" It wasn't an uncomfortable sensation, but even in Wonderland, she'd never *jumped into a painting*. She carefully pushed one arm in, then her other arm, then took a breath and stepped inside entirely.

The world changed around her.

She gasped, suddenly standing in a street lined with market stalls. The people walking down the street looked so alive, she couldn't believe they were in a picture.

"Vegetables!" a vendor cried from nearby. "Fresh vegetables and fruit here!"

"Come on—you can try before you buy!"

She had so many questions about this…painted?… street, but she didn't have the time. She ran down the road.

She soon came to a big street, just like Jericho had described. She turned right and kept walking, but saw no incoming, dead-end intersection. After about three blocks, she saw walls, but all of them still left open pathways.

"How far does this go?" she wondered aloud. She trusted Jericho's advice and kept walking, but the road just stretched on straight before her…never changing.

"This is so weird…"

"What's the matter, miss?" someone asked from nearby. "Looking for something?"

"She may be lost. It's a pretty big town."

Alice stopped, her lips curling into a frown. She felt crazy asking people inside a painting for directions, but eh. Wonderland *was* crazy.

"I…heard there was a T-intersection if you keep going this way?"

One of the friendly men waved a hand. "Oh yeah, I know what you're talking about. There *used* to be one, but it disappeared."

"Huh?" she blurted. "You mean…the *wall* vanished?"

"You got it. Somebody painted over it with sky-colored paint. It sure caused problems for us!"

As the men wandered off, Alice ran a hand through her hair. Her eyes flicked back and forth.

If I try to go back now, she thought worriedly, *I might get lost, since I don't know where I am. But I can't stay here forever, either.*

The *last* thing she wanted was to walk until she collapsed inside a piece of art. With no other options, Alice found a corner in the blind spot of a building and turned down that road.

She proceeded down the narrow road at a trot, her eyes on the ground. She saw light dimly reflecting off of what looked like tiles.

"A picture frame!" she breathed.

She couldn't see much, but the light spilling up from the ground looked much like the frame she'd seen in the museum. She held her breath and dove in.

Her body's orientation took another drastic change; it was like gravity itself spun and twisted her around. She slumped to the ground, her mind whirling, and tried not to be sick.

Where am I?!

She swallowed bile and forced her head up. Her eyes widened.

She'd never been to this place in the Country of Diamonds, but she knew it immediately. Grave markers stretched in a solemn row before her, amidst patches of thin, scraggly grass. She saw piles of soil—newly upturned ground.

This was Jericho's graveyard, in the same territory as the art museum. She cursed her luck for dropping her *right where the Hatters were attacking*.

In a panic, Alice tried to stand, but her legs turned to jelly beneath her. She gurgled as the world spun again, her senses warping around her.

*Not again! Not **now**!*

It was that same dizziness that had plagued her since coming to the Country of Diamonds. And this time, it was stronger than ever; she couldn't even sit up.

She spilled weakly against the ground, her arms splaying out in front of her. Her palms slid across mud as she collapsed, the raw scent of grass filling her nostrils.

"Who's there?!"

"Hey, there's a girl over here!"

The last things she heard were the cries of unfamiliar men.

"Stunning work, as always."

"What do you expect, when my sister dear does nothing but *bark orders* from the sidelines?"

"We only wish to keep Our lazy brother on his toes. You should thank Us."

The conversation was faint, as if it could fade into the night breeze. Alice moaned and lifted her head.

The graveyard had disappeared; she lay in a beautifully manicured, miniature garden. Green ivy and leaves cut through the vivid red of roses. Even the breeze caressing her body seemed to shimmer.

"......"

It was the secret rose garden in Hatter Mansion— the one limited to two special visitors. Nostalgia welled up in Alice just as realization dropped her stomach.

This is...a dream.

Alice was in the Country of Diamonds. Even if she'd moved back to Hearts or Clover, it was *way* too convenient for her to land here. Her eyes followed the voices.

Vivaldi, Queen of Hearts, and the Mad Hatter, Blood Dupre, sat at a nearby table. They shot loving barbs at each other and seemed to overlook Alice entirely.

"B-Blood?" she whispered, her voice a tiny croak. "Vivaldi...?"

They didn't respond. A weak smile pulled at her lips.

She didn't like intruding on their private time, anyway.

I could only dirty this beautiful place.

Alice loved beautiful things. It was why she'd fallen in love with this location, where she could see two beautiful people against a perfect backdrop. A small, exquisite space, close yet distant from her, cut off from the rest of the world.

She watched Blood walk to a nearby vine and twist his wrist in it. He twisted over and over, the vine sliding up his arm.

"Blood," she breathed. "Why...did you..."

"Why did you let me come here?"

The Blood of Hearts and Clover had invited her into this sacred place. She had no idea why. And even though he'd hit on her and made rude comments, he'd never once touched her in a genuinely sexual way. Just little teases. Just some goading that riled her up and made him smile wickedly. He didn't mean it.

He'd never pinned her down like the Blood in the Country of Diamonds.

He'd never had reason to touch her like that. Or maybe he had reason *not* to touch her.

She closed her eyes. When she opened them, Vivaldi was gone. Only Blood remained at a short distance, that vine of roses snaking around his arm. He spoke in a low, breathy voice, like he was talking to himself.

"Blood...?"

Her reedy voice barely made a sound, but he

suddenly reacted.

"Alice."

He called her name as if in response, and her heart thundered in her chest. But she didn't think he was actually answering her.

And that wasn't his voice. The Blood of Hearts and Clover never called to her like that.

He looked exactly the same—his suit, his hat, the shape of his face were just like the old Blood, down to the tiniest detail.

But his eyes were different. He was strong, but seemed too young to use that strength to the fullest. His gaze was hot.

This was Blood Dupre of the Country of Diamonds.

The moment she realized that…the garden faded away.

She jolted awake somewhere dark, her cheek crushed against a cold floor.

Something had been tied over her eyes…a blindfold? She felt cords binding her arms and feet.

"Where am I?" she breathed. When she tried to move, something hard rammed into her side.

"Ow!"

"Hold still," somebody snarled. "Make any funny moves and you're dead!"

Judging from the unfamiliar voice, someone stood over her—and had probably kicked her. She wanted to scream at him, but she knew that would be stupid. She bit the inside of her cheek.

She remembered the voices she'd heard before passing out. Were they the people attacking Jericho? Had they captured her?

Then...they can't be Hatters, she thought quickly. *Even **they** wouldn't treat me like this.* Who exactly had attacked the graveyard?

She felt unharmed, and she was tied up, so someone had decided she was too useful to kill. She couldn't suppress a sigh at her calculating thoughts.

I guess I've really gotten used to this world. She didn't know if that made her glad or depressed.

Someone shouted in the distance. Male voices hissed at each other over her.

"Here they come...!"

Someone shoved something hard and metallic against her head—the barrel of a gun. Her face distorted in pain.

"Don't move!" her captor ordered as he ground the barrel into her skull. "Whoever it is, he can't save you that easily!"

She frantically shook her head. "No!" she gasped.

"Shut up! I told you not to—gah!"

A gunshot rang out, cutting him off. His grip went slack and the gun fell from her head as she heard him crumple to the floor.

"You should take your own advice and shut your mouth!"

"Th-the Gravekeep—"

WHAM

Something heavy hit something else, and the man finally went silent. Alice recoiled from the tangy scent of iron as strong fingers gripped her arm.

"Are you all right, Alice?"

"J-Jericho?"

He hauled her to a sitting position and pulled down her blindfold. The light dazzled her for a second, but she blinked until her sight returned.

Jericho's prim suit was gone. The man before her, armed with a gun, was the fearsome leader of the Gravekeeper's territory.

He shook his head and started untying her. "Forgive me," he murmured quickly. "I didn't know the painting had been vandalized. And now I've gotten you mixed up in my problems… I have to get you out of here."

"B-but they're after you, right?" she argued. "I'll just slow you down!"

"I'll be fine. This was my fault to begin with."

She let him pull her to her feet. They ran to the exit; she tried to get him to leave in another direction, but he refused. He dragged her along behind him.

Sure enough, Faceless started popping up, shouting and pointing at the territory leader in their midst. Alice gasped and ran to keep up.

"It's the damn Gravekeeper!" a voice shouted.

"Say your prayers, Jericho Bermuda!"

"You're going down right now!"

Jericho flipped up his revolver.

The Faceless charged with guns, knives, even explosives—but Jericho just fired round after round into their shrieking bodies. They never even got close. He glanced back at Alice as his gun boomed.

"People underestimate me because I'm already dead," he said coolly. "But they won't stop me *here*."

"Dammit," someone snarled. "Take him down! Now!"

Jericho was a lone man against countless adversaries, but he didn't even look strained. Alice knew the Role-Holders in Wonderland could just mow down the Faceless, so Jericho seemed as powerful as the other territory leaders. A question floated to the top of her mind as she ran.

How can he be this strong if he's "already dead"?

Jericho stopped, leaving Alice to catch her breath. He gestured with his gun.

"If we head down that way, we'll get to the exit fast. Sorry, but I'm going to ask you to accompany me a little farther." He cocked his gun into a ready position, then held his other hand out to Alice.

"Uh, Jericho? You—huh?!"

He suddenly jerked his hand back and instead shoved her, using the force to propel himself in the opposite direction. Alice stumbled back as the Gravekeeper dove into a roll, bullets zipping through the air where he'd been standing. The gunshots came from the location of the exit.

Jericho grunted and whipped up his gun. "Pretty small-minded of you," he shouted sourly.

"I'd *love* for you to suggest something more efficient. I've got future plans I should be getting to, since I actually *have* a future, unlike you."

Alice froze. A white figure emerged from the darkness, his footsteps heavy. She made out the shape of a top hat and saw enemy blood spattered across his suit.

"Blood?!"

Blood scowled, smoke rising from the barrel of his gun. "Why are you so surprised?" he snapped.

Her defenses rose up automatically. "What are you even doing here?!" she shouted back. *And why do you always have to argue with me?!*

She didn't think she was important enough to him to merit a rescue. In fact, he was the very man who had said the Blood of Hearts and Clover, who had called Alice "precious," was frustrated and repressed.

He made a beeline for her, sucked his teeth, and

grabbed her arm.

"You're supposed to get my permission any time you want to leave the mansion. Don't even pretend that you didn't know that!"

"No, but I told the maid… A-and she passed it along, didn't she?!"

The Mad Hatter laughed in her face.

He suddenly flashed a smile that she knew well from the *old* Blood. Somehow both degenerate and alluring—a fearless smile.

"You didn't get my *permission*, young lady. You never even asked me directly! You've got guts to breach a contract with me; in the Mafia world, that can get you *killed*."

"Ow! Hey—mmph!"

He grabbed her roughly into an embrace and kissed her. His hot mouth bit against hers.

In the resulting shock, she could only watch as he stepped around her, blocking her from Jericho. She heard the ring of Jericho's gunshot.

She tensed, but the bullet zipped nowhere near them. A warning shot. Was Jericho trying to drive them away?

Blood turned his back on Jericho's barrage of bullets, clearly unconcerned, and lifted Alice up into his arms like a bride over the threshold.

"We should go," he hummed. "I'll deal out your punishment later, in my own sweet time…got it?"

"P-punishment? Ah!"

There was no time to question the ominous promise. With a dramatic flap of his jacket, the Mad Hatter ran into the night, Alice clinging to his neck for dear life.

ACT 7

What I Would Exchange Here and Now

Alice didn't know how they got out. And it felt like a long distance between the graveyard and Hatter territory...but Blood ran the entire way, holding Alice tightly against his chest.

He obviously hadn't invaded Jericho's territory alone; as they made the trip back, Hatter mobsters ran out of the woodwork to join them, shouting and reinforcing the lone Blood in his escape. Alice was relieved to see friendly faces, but at the same time, questions bubbled up in her throat.

Once they arrived back home, Blood carried her to his room and kicked the door in. He finally put her down to sink into one of his sofas.

Alice sat up nervously and looked up at him. His hair and clothes were disheveled and dirty, but he didn't even look *winded*.

She swallowed.

"Blood…why did you come?" she asked quietly. "That was Jericho's fight. With *his* enemies."

"You catch on fast, young lady. I should've made you my chief of staff instead of my librarian."

Alice's shoulders drooped in dismay; she didn't want him to make fun of her. As Blood made a theatrical gesture, she let out a frustrated breath.

"Let's get one thing straight, Blood. Jericho had come to save me when you—huh?!"

Her words devolved into a yelp as he suddenly pushed her back into the sofa. He crawled on top of her, the couch creaking slightly beneath them.

"Alice," he murmured. "I agree that we should get something *straight*."

Frustration snaked through her veins, driving her hands up to ball against his looming chest. "Blood!"

He'd snatched her away from Jericho, the man who'd *actually* saved her, and kissed her right in front of him. She was humiliated.

"I don't get you!" Alice cried. "Are you just making fun of me again?!"

"No. I just decided to *make* you give up on all the others, no matter who they are or how you feel about them."

"What does that even mean?!" She glared as hard as she could, but it didn't faze those blue-green eyes.

"Let me make this *very clear*," he said evenly, his voice a low rumble. "I don't care if it's some other Mafia boss or even another version of myself—I don't have it in me to hand you over to anybody. I'll never, *ever* give away the woman I love."

Alice froze. Her mouth fell open in shock.

"Love?" she whispered without thinking.

"You may be in love with the other Blood Dupre, but I'm keeping you here with me. For good."

"……"

Alice could only stare at him for a long moment, stupefied. Blood stared into her eyes, his ruffled hair brushing his face like tousled midnight.

She tried to organize the spinning thoughts in her head.

"Blood… You don't understand."

"I understand fine. You have stronger feelings for *that* Blood than you do for me." He smiled darkly, like he'd never doubted his guess. "And those intense, lingering feelings are why you always argue with me. My similarity to him repulses you. And I get that, but I'm disappointed."

"Like I said—you don't understand! I *like* that Blood, but not as a lover!"

She and the old Blood had never crossed the line of friendship. She didn't know how many different ways she could say it.

Blood's brow furrowed. "So you admit that you like him."

"What do you want from me, Blood?! I'd be lying if I said I hated him!"

"You had to be in love with him," Blood insisted. "You're an elegant girl and he was an underworld Mob boss. A fiend."

Alice doubted he would believe her if she told him *because I thought I was in a dream.* That that had made her brave and reckless in the Country of Hearts…and had led to everything she valued by the time she stopped thinking she was asleep.

But since this Blood didn't know how her life in Wonderland had started, his mouth tightened in dissatisfaction.

"If you were in love," he said, "I could understand it. Even a bright woman like you can make a mistake of the heart. But I don't believe it was just friendship."

"But it *was!*"

"When I kissed you, you didn't resist. You let your guard down because you had feelings for that Blood…and I share his body." He clenched his teeth. "If you're not even doing it consciously…that's even worse."

"Blood…!"

Why wouldn't he understand? Why wouldn't he believe her?!

She felt borderline rage radiating from her face. He just barked a wicked laugh.

"Did you show *that* expression to the man you love? I hope so—that's exactly what I want."

"ARGH!" she roared. If he hadn't been crushing her arms into the sofa with his weight, she would've torn out her hair.

"What are you so upset for?"

She was about to screech a rebuttal, but then stopped. She felt the anger drain out of her as doubt crept up in its place.

*Why **am** I so upset?*

Why did she care that *this* Blood misunderstood her relationship with the old Blood? This was Blood's M.O. Even in Hearts and Clover, he'd constantly teased her about being in love with Peter in Heart Castle, even though he was dead wrong.

And the old Blood hadn't *just* teased her about Peter—he'd teased her about practically every man in Wonderland. She'd always told him to shut up before moving on. It didn't *frustrate* her like this. It didn't fill her chest with the tension she now felt tightening around her heart.

She stared up at him. Blood stared back.

And this Blood, with the face she knew, with the intimidation and sharp wit she'd known in other countries…he stared at her now with different eyes. And with an expression she *didn't* know well.

Those eyes searched hers, exposing her doubts and trapping her in a blue-green prison. She saw a hint of helplessness behind his gaze—like he was frustrated at not getting what he wanted.

She saw the true feelings that he always hid behind biting sarcasm and an unruffled countenance. His real intentions were *here*. And that was why she'd recognized him in her dream in the rose garden… only the Blood of Diamonds had these eyes.

And…they were the eyes she wanted.

Oh my God.

It was why she'd gotten so upset when he accused her of loving the other Blood. It was why she couldn't just brush him off when he voiced all his doubts.

She hated that this realization had taken her so long. But she didn't let a curse or a groan escape with her heavy sigh; instead, a wry smile floated on her lips.

I'm in love with Blood of the Country of Diamonds.

His lips tightened slightly. "Just admit it," he rasped. "You're in love with a version of Blood Dupre."

She rolled her eyes to the ceiling. "I…am…"

She felt a sense of doom settle on her shoulders

with the realization. How could she be attracted to a man like this? A stubborn, cutting, jealous, egotistical, and overly analytical Mob boss? His personality was basically a list of negatives. She was so disappointed in her taste that she fell into silence.

What a headache.

"The Blood of Hearts and Clover has always been important to me," she murmured. "And he always will be. I wish he were here to hear this."

Blood's body tightened over her; she shook her head to cut off his raging jealousy.

"But he's *not* the one I love, Blood. You are."

"…What?"

Blood's dumbfounded voice leaked from his lips. He looked off-balance, like she'd dodged his best right hook.

The old Blood wouldn't have revealed such an open face. She felt an urge to smile.

"I never had any idea what he thought of me. But I still knew he didn't hate me…and I'm pretty sure he *liked* me. But I can't tell you if it was the same 'love' that you just spoke of. He never told me."

The old Blood hadn't gone near her until he'd fully accepted her—and then he'd still held her at a safe distance, even if his affection had seemed too deep for simple "interest." He'd considered her special. But how?

Maybe that Blood had been looking for steady, unwavering love, and she was an Outsider who could vanish at any time. Maybe he didn't want to *burden* her with his feelings. Or maybe he'd been hoping for a different kind of love, or something she couldn't give him. With them both in different countries now, Alice had no way of finding out.

He'd let her into his rose garden in Hatter Mansion—a juxtaposition of calm against cruelty. Like him. She'd been special enough to him for him to throw open those doors. Maybe he himself hadn't known the reason.

But he'd cradled her in his secret world, and Alice had liked that. She'd never wanted more from him… and she prayed their relationship never changed.

She looked up into the gaze of the man breathing heavily on her lips.

"You're a Mafia boss," she murmured at last.

"You're power-hungry, stubborn, prideful to a fault, hard to understand, and you kiss people in public.

"But...you tried to get close to me. You tried to find out about the real me. That's probably the biggest difference between you and the old Blood. And that's why I...fell for you."

She knew what kind of person Blood Dupre was. But even knowing that, she wanted to know the Blood in front of her better. The younger Blood who didn't keep his distance, even in a land of distrust and violent enemies. When *this* Blood had said he was going to investigate her, she'd felt, deep down in her heart...a tiny bloom of happiness.

He stared at her and didn't say a word.

Alice let out a breath and scowled. "What, Blood? Are you seriously going to make me do all the talking?"

Blood blinked a few times, as if regaining his thoughts. "I just...didn't expect that," he murmured. "You stunned me speechless."

"You're blushing," she teased.

Blood screwed up his face and sucked his teeth.

"Shut up. I didn't think you even *liked* me, let

alone…" His finger gently brushed up the side of her face, and she was reminded of his soft touch when he'd nursed her arm. His finger slowly twisted into a lock of her hair, wrapping the strands around and around.

Alice couldn't believe they'd been fighting a second ago.

She slanted her mouth. "You didn't know whether I liked you or not, and you still…kissed me in front of Jericho?"

"Doing that made it more difficult for you to go back to him." He hummed and twisted her hair. "Two birds with one stone."

"Ugh. You're an awful man."

"Good—I can't keep this job *unless* I'm an awful man."

She smiled at him. Blood chuckled back.

The words weren't sweet, but she felt a sudden hunger for his warmth. She slid her arms around the lean frame pressing down on her and tilted her mouth up.

"Ah…"

"…mm…"

The kiss was nothing like their first. As her lips caught with his, once then over and over as heat built up inside her, her mind went white. She closed her eyes.

His own arms snaked under her and up her back as he pushed down on top of her. Crushed up against his body as his mouth moved against hers, fear suddenly gripped her pounding heart.

"Mm—wait," she breathed, the panic pushing words into his mouth. She couldn't think of a good excuse. "Our clothes will get…wrinkled."

He grunted, the sound a wet vibration against her mouth. "I envy your ability to think right now."

Alice gasped as one broad hand slid over her body, caressing her through the thin barrier of her clothes. He slid his mouth off hers and instead chuckled a low rumble into her ear.

She wasn't mentally prepared for this.

"W-wait, Blood—"

"You said you loved me, right? Maybe the other Blood Dupre couldn't catch you, but I will."

"Catch me? You… Ah!"

She felt heat in a risky part of Blood's body and

her voice jumped an octave.

She wanted to run. She wanted to bury herself in her safe, familiar anxieties.

But his low voice changed her mind.

"I've caught you, and now you're *mine*—more precious to me than anything or anyone. I'm the Blood Dupre who will take you away."

The heat of his words melted her thoughts away. She felt drunk on the urgent, heavy desire that drove his hand around her body.

She let that hand wander.

"S-stupid," she gasped, but it turned into a moan.

"Having fun yet?"

Alice looked up from the revelers at the Garden Party and turned her head. Blood caught her eyes, a small twitch at the corner of his mouth.

She nodded and placed her drink on a nearby table. "But…this is the last Survey Meeting, right? And you're a participant—how long can you afford to be hanging around here?"

Blood shrugged. Excited Diamonds citizens bustled around him, enjoying the final party hosted by their castle.

"Without all four leaders there, they can't start. Let them wait."

She scowled. "That's unbelievably rude."

"Meh."

Alice sighed. With the mood Blood was in, he didn't care about the final results of the third Survey Meeting. But…he'd come in last, then second-to-last in the other meetings. That meant he'd already decided which of his forces to use at the end, right?

Unless he's just blowing the whole thing off now.

She tugged him toward the exit, and he finally complied. Their path took them right by the ticket windows…where two young men noticed them and shrieked their greetings.

"Boss~!" Dee cried as he ran up with his brother. "Perfect timing! It's the last meeting, so you oughta show us your hand!"

"Brother's right!" Dum yelled. "You gotta help us make up for what we lost last time! If we lose anymore, we're gonna cry ourselves to sleep!"

Alice grimaced. "Boys, that isn't just cheating, it's out-and-out fraud."

But the twins didn't understand "morals," and they just got louder.

"Don't get cheap in the last stupid round! Boss, we wanna rake it in on every bet! Stakes are real high now!"

"Ya can't hold back—not this time! Tell 'im, Big Sis—this is for a good cause! You don't wanna waste our money!"

Alice winced and slid a finger in her ear. The twins ran back to the windows, taking their noise with them.

But for better or worse...they don't treat me differently now that they know about Blood and me. They're the only ones who still look at me the same way.

Her treatment in the Hatter Mansion had changed a little since becoming Blood's girlfriend. The guards trailing her had changed to "escorts," and the watchful eyes of the mansion's residents had softened considerably.

It was *Elliot's* behavior that actually bothered her.

She swore to get him to stop calling her "Sister."

She pursed her lips. "It *is* the final Survey Meeting," she admitted after a moment. "Maybe I'll make just one last bet."

"Huh? I didn't expect something like *that* to come out of your mouth." Blood looked genuinely surprised, and Alice couldn't help but laugh at his face.

"True. But we don't know if there will ever be another Survey Meeting, so I'd better get the full experience under my belt. I just won't bet the farm like Dee and Dum."

She lowered her voice. "Besides," she added, quiet enough that he wouldn't hear her. "I never know when I might move again."

She knew that in the next move, she might be the only one to switch countries again…and she'd leave everything in Diamonds behind. That possibility renewed her desire to make as many good memories with Blood as she could.

Blood adjusted his hat and said nothing.

"Now," she went on. "What should I do this time? Last time I bet on Hatter Mansion coming in third, but…maybe you'll come in second?"

She looked up at the window bulletin board; her eyes scanned the list of bet combinations and the predicted winnings of each. As the twins had said, Hatter Mansion wasn't favored—clearly the result of Blood's poor performance in the first two meetings.

Blood remained silent by her side while she hummed over the possibilities. He eventually let out a breath.

"Alice."

She turned to look up at him…but he'd already clutched her hand and slid something into it.

The surprise softened her hand. She had to scramble to keep from dropping the top hat she now held.

"Huh?" She blinked. It wasn't the hat he wore now—the one that matched the tailored black suit he wore to Survey Meetings. This was the hat he wore with his everyday clothes. The design was exactly the same, including the decorative card, roses, and feathers. The only difference was the playing card had a pattern separated into four colors.

"Is this…your normal hat?" She ran her fingers along the brim. "Why are you giving it to me?"

"It's for a bet of my own."

She paused. "I thought only regular citizens had the right to bet. The leaders can bet, too?"

Blood laughed and tapped the hat in her hand. "This is just a *personal* wager," he explained. "A game."

"Blood, what can you win by betting a hat?"

He smiled. He took her shoulder, drew her close, and whispered in her ear.

"I'm going to bet that my territory comes in first. When that happens, the hat is yours."

His words sounded like the plot of a mischievous little boy, but his tone was serious.

Alice frowned. "That doesn't make sense. That would mean that if you win, you don't get any prize."

"Of *course* I'll win a prize. I win the one who won the hat." He raised an eyebrow. "That's worth winning, right?"

Heat flooded her face. "W-wait, then you're saying… H-hold on a second, Blood!"

But he was already walking toward the arena—

saying his piece and walking off, like the twins. Alice cradled the silken hat against her chest and scrambled to follow.

When they reached their area, Blood stopped her before she could sit down in her regular seat. "No, Alice. Not there."

"Why not? It's where I sat before."

"Before," he repeated with emphasis. "But this time, your seat is *here.*"

Alice balked at the front row seat beside his. She'd felt self-conscious enough in the *second* row! She frantically shook her head.

"Don't even joke, Blood. I'm an Outsider, and I'm not even one of your employees. What are you trying to make me do?!"

"There's no need to be shy," he drawled. "Not with our relationship."

"Nngh…"

If this had been before their big confession, she could've gotten out of this with a cold smile. It was a lot harder to argue once she'd told the man she loved him.

She still hesitated. "But…"

Elliot, in his regular seat, threw her one of his new smiles.

"Go ahead, Sister! Blood says it's okay, so we've got your back."

She scowled at him. "You're not helping, Elliot."

She had a feeling none of the other Hatters would come to her aid, either. Still worried she was breaking an unwritten rule, she lowered herself into the seat. She twitched in discomfort.

"It's about to start, young lady. And this is the last session—so try to enjoy it?"

"It's because I *want* to enjoy it that I wish I wasn't sitting here," she grumbled. "I don't want to be in any spotlight!"

Before Blood could retort, the familiar announcer appeared. He threw up an arm.

"Welcome to the final Survey Meeting!" he boomed. "Are all of you excited?!"

No. Alice shrank down in her seat as the crowds roared around her. She had the feeling Blood had dragged her to this seat for some sort of plan. She threw him a look through half-lidded eyes.

"What exactly do you expect me to do here?"

"You refused to assist me in the first Survey Meeting," he replied, an infuriating calm under his ridiculous words. "So you'll assist me now. You'll choose the final card."

"…Huh?"

"No, not 'huh.' This is the last meeting to settle our standing, Alice. I want you to conclude it."

She leapt out of her chair, but he grabbed her arm. She struggled as he pulled her back down onto the seat.

"No!" she hissed. "Let go of me!"

"It's too late to run."

"I have *no idea* how forces are used here, Blood! And I'm not a territory leader—so I couldn't do it if I wanted to!"

"It's not hard. You just put your hand on the controls and bring up a mental image of the force you want. Anybody can do that much."

Alice threw up a hand in frustration. "You're not listening to me! Is this another one of your plots?"

His smile was cool and collected, which set off Alice's warning alarms. The more placid Blood was, the more suspicious. And when she glared at him, he just calmly brushed her off.

The other territory leaders, meanwhile, finished their plays. From the Castle to the Gravekeeper to the Station, each team showed their forces...leaving only Hatter Mansion. Alice squirmed in her seat.

Blood made no attempt to move, inciting louder cries from the crowds around them. Alice could feel the tension rising, all part of a good show... Unless he wasn't planning to break it.

Argh!

Blood leveled those blue-green eyes on her.

"Everyone's waiting for the results, Alice. And now, so am I." He opened a palm toward her. "Give me your hand."

Her anxiety and frustration exploding in her gut, Alice slapped her hand into his. "D-don't blame me if I screw this up!" she blurted. "What forces do you even have left?"

She knew there were a total of five possible powers, and they'd already used one in each of the other meetings. Once a force had been used, it couldn't be used again. Blood wanted her to choose a card without being able to see what was in the hand.

Blood hummed. "You want to know what's left? I'd rather hear what you *think* is left, but then you might panic, hm?"

"Don't you dare!"

Blood ignored her glare and leaned in to whisper in her ear. "I've used natural resources and technology, not necessarily in that order."

Alice licked her dry lips. "Okay. So I should choose from one of the others?"

That meant population, economics, and military were left. She *wished* she could give it more thought, but there was no time...and she knew nothing of those forces in Hatter territory, let alone within the *other* territories. She couldn't compare things she didn't understand.

She paused. "Do...do you want me to put out a winning card?" she whispered. "Or would you rather I put out something weaker?"

He shrugged. "Pick whatever you want. If you want to *win,* use a strong card. If you want to hide our strengths, then choose a weak one."

"Then...you're really leaving it up to me?" She was starting to feel stupid for taking the choice so seriously. Her shoulders drooped.

"I told you, Alice—this is just entertainment. What's the harm in trusting your last hand to blind luck?" His eyes glittered. "And I know you're a lucky girl."

"Just…promise me you won't blame me for what happens. I mean it!"

Blood was putting the entire outcome, whether they won or lost, completely in her control. And when she thought of it that way, her mind opened up.

Population, economics, military strength. Alice recalled as much of the Hatter Mansion as she could. The other leaders had made their choices; her eyes fell on the sand flowing into the glass receptacles.

Make a choice.

"Um…population," she murmured at last.

"All right." Blood tugged her hand to the control stand, then let it go. "Go for it."

Alice slowly lowered her hand onto the control stand. Blood placed his gloved hand over hers.

"Remember," he whispered. "Keep your hand on the panel and just *think* of your chosen force. Then the stand will transmit it and the sand will react."

"Okay…"

"Just concentrate, Alice. I'll control the sand."

She curled her fingers on the stand and thought of the people of Hatter territory.

She remembered the weary citizens, worn down with constant battles. But she knew that wasn't the ultimate fate for that territory. She knew how strong the Hatters would become.

"Huh?"

Alice opened her eyes in surprise, then squinted as a light on the stand brightened. Blood pushed up closer behind her, his fingers closing over hers.

"Just stay like that, Alice. You've made the connection."

She glanced up quickly at his smile, something welling up inside her. She nodded and closed her eyes again, her mind returning to their population.

"The sand has finally started to pour!" the announcer cried from elsewhere. "The climax of the Survey Meeting!"

Alice heard cheers, laughs, chaos swelling around her. But she tuned it all out…

And thought of all those people under Blood.

"Diamond Castle won the first meeting!" the announcer declared, his voice leaking into Alice's ears. "And the Gravekeeper's territory came out on top in the second! Which territory will take the laurels in the final round?!"

Alice anxiously gritted her teeth. Just thinking that Hatter Mansion might go through all three meetings without taking first position filled her chest with complicated emotions.

She finally opened her eyes. All four glass chambers were filled with sand, although the Hatter level was low and the other three seemed about even. She saw a slow overhead trickle in varying strengths across them.

"Is...the sand still flowing?" she breathed.

"Yes. In all four."

Blood said he can control the sand. She saw the incoming streams increase, then decrease, riling up the audience. The leaders were trying to make it *fun.* Alice remembered what Blood had said about the Survey Meeting as entertainment.

The green sand for the Station finally stopped. The receptacle was almost full, but so were the others. And the other three streams kept going.

Nightmare cried out in frustration. "No!" he wailed.

He'd had the most land area right from the start, but he couldn't stop the other territories from adding to their totals. And now he was out.

The Castle and the Gravekeeper's territory had slowed their streams…but then, suddenly, Hatter Mansion's sand burst into a heavier flow. The crowd roared.

"What's this?!" the announcer cried. "Look at Hatter Mansion!"

Alice watched, her heart in her throat, as their receptacle rapidly filled with blue sand until it was even with the other two leaders. Then it surpassed them, reaching the top of the glass chamber. Then it *kept going.*

Cracks raced along the glass as the blue sand filled the chamber to bursting. Alice recoiled in alarm.

"Huh?!"

With a loud, explosive *CRACK,* the front face of the vessel broke open, sending a spray of blue to fan across the air. Sand spilled out into the arena, causing the announcer to leap out of the way in surprise.

"What?!" he blurted. "It's…gone into overflow! What does this mean? The Hatter's sand broke through the measurement chamber!" He blinked. "Oh—and the Castle and Gravekeeper's flows have both stopped!"

A hush fell over the crowd, followed by a ripple of uncomfortable murmuring. Men started to gather around the announcer.

"How could the receptacle break?"

"Has that ever happened at a Survey Meeting before?"

"I bet on the Mad Hatter! What happens to my bet now…?"

The impromptu committee around the announcer didn't last long. After a minute of discussion, the announcer nodded his head and turned back to the crowd.

"We've made a decision!" He threw his head back and bellowed, "The winner of the third Survey Meeting is definitely Hatter Mansion!"

The crowd went *wild*. Alice heard cheers and whistles mixed with booming complaints; the roar engulfed the entire Coliseum as she stared, amazed, at the broken glass receptacle. She slowly slid her hand off the control panel. "Your population force… was that *huge?*" she asked Blood in a daze.

It was so much more than the other territories. And why had the sand kept going, even when the structure couldn't handle it? Why didn't the stream just stop when the receptacle was full?

A disgusted grunt cut off her thoughts. She turned to the next group over and into the cold stare of the Black Rabbit.

"They cheated," Sidney said thinly from behind his queen. "I wish I could prove it."

And it wasn't just him. Nightmare hunched his shoulders; Gray and Boris stared. Jericho watched Blood from the Gravekeeper section, Julius sighing behind him.

The young version of Ace, still sitting, just kicked his dangling legs. He tilted his head at Julius.

"Julius?" he asked. "Is this, y'know…*that?*"

"The rules don't cover it," Julius answered evenly.

"I don't approve, but I can't say it's illegal, either."

"Seems kinda unfair."

"......"

Alice figured they were blaming her, but why? At a loss, Alice looked up at Blood...but he was just watching the other territories from over the top of her head, a wicked smile on his lips.

The announcer stepped up again. "And that ends our final Survey Meeting! Will you help us close the events, Your Majesty?"

The Queen of Diamonds pursed her lips, narrowing her eyes slightly in dissatisfaction.

"The Mad Hatter is a tricky man. He didn't dirty his own hands, but the act was dirty." Crysta sighed, as if exasperated but not angry, and stood from her chair. She arranged her long skirts before turning to the stage.

"Rules are rules," she announced, "and they indicate that this Survey Meeting is over. However, we'll see to it that the same thing doesn't happen again. Right, Sidney?"

Sidney nodded, his voice ice. "As Her Majesty says."

A shiver ran down Alice's spine. Blood shrugged at the queen, and she proceeded to ignore him.

At the queen's command, the Coliseum began to calm down. The last of the blue sand trickled quietly through broken glass.

Alice walked down a deserted corridor with Blood, their footsteps echoing in the ghostly silence. She gripped Blood's wagered top hat in her hands.

The underground hallway led far ahead of them and into darkness—a path from the arena to the waiting room. Crysta, as host, could have teleported them back...but Blood had refused this time, sending Elliot and the twins ahead of him. Judging by the completely abandoned hall, "walking" wasn't a popular choice.

Blood had said he wanted to "enjoy the feeling of being a winner with the young lady awhile longer," but she knew that was an excuse. Alice took a breath and looked up at him.

Her confusion was driving her crazy.

"Blood?" she asked, her voice careful. "What happened back there?"

"I'm surprised you have to ask. Hatter Mansion wound up in first place."

"Don't try to pull one over on me! Why did Sidney say you cheated?"

"Is there any real need to worry about the ranting of an animal?"

"Blood!" She scowled at him; she wouldn't let him distract her with a smoke-and-mirrors act.

"More importantly," he drawled, completely ignoring her pleas, "I won the bet, and I've warned you about *punishment* for breaching a contract with me. Put on your prize."

"Huh? Whoa!"

He pulled the hat from her hands and dropped it on her head with a soft *clump*. It was way too big for her; it covered half her face, and she had to push up the brim so it wouldn't block her eyes.

But when she lifted the dark band from her vision, Blood's face was suddenly very close to hers. Her protest died in her throat.

"Like I thought," he rumbled. "It suits you. Very cute, Alice."

She grimaced. "Yeah, right," she grunted. His flattery about an oversized, flamboyant hat engulfing her head was too much—even for him.

But she paused at the genuine happiness in his voice.

The hat stank of tobacco smoke. The other Blood—of Hearts and Clover—smelled like the tea and roses from his secret garden. The comparison made the Blood beside her seem downright barbaric.

If he'd done this a little while ago, I would've thrown this hat back in his face. She would've been afraid to even touch a hat so suffused with smoke.

But now, knowing that it was his…she delicately cradled the brim with her fingers.

"You promised," he reminded her. "So take it. It's yours now."

She nodded, keeping the huge brim up with her hand. "Yeah… I'll be careful not to lose it. This settles the bet, Blood."

Blood answered her with an affirmative sound.

Seeing his gentle face made her so happy, but at

the same time, a creeping sadness threatened to ruin it. She swallowed hard.

The closer we become, the more anxious I get. And I could still "move." She dropped her eyes to the floor.

If she had to leave Blood some day, at least she'd have these memories, right? She wanted to be as close to him as possible in the time they had together.

*But I don't want to move. I want to stay **here**.*

"You really did it this time, Hatter!"

Alice jumped. Heavy clumps of leather shoes echoed in the empty hallway.

"Wh…"

A familiar, broad shape appeared in the darkness ahead. He walked alone, without his followers, his piercing gaze leveled on Blood.

Jericho.

The limited light threw shadows over his face; his muscled form and severe expression made Alice recoil in fear. But when his eyes fell to her, his face softened slightly.

"I feel sorry for you," he told her, his deep voice tinged with something. "Looking at you…I'm guessing you didn't know you were an accomplice in a scam."

Alice went rigid. "*Accomplice?* What are you talking about?"

"So you really don't know? You just—"

"State your business, Gravekeeper," Blood interrupted. He stepped in front of Alice. "We're busy."

Jericho's face darkened at Blood's tone. Alice could finally see the Mafia boss lurking behind Jericho's kindness.

"The girl wants an explanation," he growled. "I'm trying to give her one."

"How thoughtful of you. Put that *diligence* into polishing your gravestones or something."

Jericho clenched his teeth. "Back off," he warned.

Alice swallowed. "Then…the thing in the arena really happened because of me?" she asked weakly.

Jericho waved a hand. "*You* didn't do anything— the Hatter used you. An Outsider is like a random number in this world. If you introduce that to *our* numbers, it's inevitable that you'll have an influence on them—that's exactly what Outsiders do here."

Blood sucked his teeth. "You've got a big mouth," he grunted.

Alice turned to Blood, her eyes wide. "Blood…?"

He let her unasked question dangle in the air for a moment. Then he shrugged.

"Look, as a territory leader, I couldn't have predicted your exact influence. An Outsider is *literally* an indeterminate factor. You were just as likely to make me *lose* big."

A high risk/high return strategy. That seemed right up Blood's alley…but it still seemed like an unusually gutsy move for the Blood in the Country of Diamonds.

"Then…why did you do it?"

When she fixed her eyes on him, he seemed at a loss for words. Then he said with a breathy sigh, "I told you before—this was a *personal* competition for me. Nobody has the right to criticize me for it." He snapped his gaze to Jericho. "Including you, Gravekeeper."

"That's big talk, Hatter. Don't forget that you just made the rest of us look like fools. You're a lazy winner to steal the spoils after someone *else* does all the work."

"Hn. Not over that yet, are you?"

Alice realized they were talking about her capture in the graveyard. God, how many times could she wrong Jericho?!

Blood snaked an arm around her shoulder. "He chose to rescue you," Blood murmured, as if reading her mind. "Don't beat yourself up over his personal decisions."

"You can't blow me off anymore, Hatter—I'm going to ask you to return that card to me now. The Survey Meetings are over, so the *other* rules end as well."

The Gravekeeper spoke in a low voice, murder in his eyes. Alice unconsciously took a step back.

"Jericho…"

Blood tightened his grip on her shoulder and pulled her against his side. As she crushed up against him, she looked up to see his face…but he seemed completely unruffled.

"You're already dead," he said evenly, "so you're not worth my time. But if you're so *anxious* for your end, I can help you out."

"......"

Alice could only watch the two glaring Mafia bosses in the empty, chilling hall. The few seconds of silence seemed to last an eternity. Alice was afraid to breathe.

Blood's arm twitched.

As if in slow motion, Jericho drew his gun as Blood's cane shifted into a pistol. She watched helplessly as they raised their weapons at each other with an echoing *chak.*

"Die!"

"Game over."

Bullets exploded from their guns, making Alice cringe back in terror. But after the single round, she heard two heavy thumps, one after the other.

"Huh?!"

She snapped her eyes past Jericho, where a prone figure lay on the ground behind him. She turned to look behind her and Blood—sure enough, another Faceless lay crumpled on the floor.

Jericho let out a breath. His face relaxed, his fearful intensity gone in an instant.

"That clears up *that* mystery," he said. "After all

the trouble of putting on the act, I expected…more of a fight."

Blood raised an eyebrow. "You know, I think you might actually be disappointed," he drawled. He turned to Alice. "Alice?"

She jerked her head up at him, then cursed herself for shaking. "Wh-what?!" she blurted. She tried to force herself to calm down.

Blood's lips curled in a self-satisfied smirk.

"As much as I love having you wrapped around me, I'd rather do it in private so *he* doesn't get a free show."

Alice, in her panic, had clung to Blood's arm in a death grip. She grunted and pulled back. She was suddenly glad for the huge hat shadowing her face— and its blush.

Blood turned back to Jericho. "Are these the last spies? You said you took care of all the rest, right?"

"Yeah. The only ones left were the ones closely tailing me. I gave them free rein for a while, but…as we figured, the final move had to be here." Jericho flipped up a hand. "Had to let them get a good dance in first."

"You do a lot of work for a dead man."

Alice pulled the hat brim down, allowing her eyes to barely peek at the men. The way they talked—up close and almost casual—she would never have believed they were rival Mafia bosses.

She started to wonder if the animosity between them had *always* been for show.

Maybe Blood let me go to the museum because I lured their mutual enemy into attacking...?

It was true that a Faceless probably couldn't attack her *directly* in the museum—not when a Role-Holder was walking around. But maybe indirectly. Maybe those sneaking Faceless had sabotaged her route inside the painting. Or maybe...

"Blood, Jericho?"

They flicked their eyes to her. Blood let out a vague chuckle, and Jericho furrowed his brow at Alice's hat.

"That thing is too big for you."

Alice sighed and tilted the brim up higher. "You think?"

"And that style doesn't suit you," Jericho said. "If you're going to wear a hat, you should...put some thought into what you pick."

Blood stepped back toward her and swept his arm around her back. "Don't worry about it," he told Jericho, although his gaze was locked on Alice. "She'll get used to it. Let's go, Alice."

He hurried her down the hallway before she knew what was happening. Her feet stumbled a little.

"But Blood—"

"It's the Gravekeeper's duty to take care of the dead. Just leave them."

That wasn't what she was worried about, but Blood ignored her stuttered questions. He led her past Jericho, past the dead Faceless lying behind him, and down the dark hallway until she and Blood were alone in that corridor again.

She didn't know how long they walked; time warped in the silence. When Blood finally stopped, she stumbled again.

She saw no sign of the waiting room up ahead. She opened her mouth to ask him, but before she knew it, he'd wrapped her up in his arms. He crushed her so close against his chest that she was dragged to her tiptoes.

"Blood?"

"I still haven't taken my winnings from my bet." His blue-green gaze burned. "But I'll take you now."

"Mm!"

He gripped her chin and roughly kissed her. Alice gasped into his mouth, her hand still gripped around the hat dangling from her head.

"The hat," she breathed against his hungry lips. "It…mm…" Heat swelled inside her as his wet mouth devoured her own.

When he finally broke the kiss, she panted, trying to regain her breath. His lips broke into a smile.

"I don't care if it's before or after you get used to your hat. You're mine now…and I won't let you go."

"Blood…"

Maybe he'd already realized that a move could tear her away someday. She tightened her jaw.

I wish I could promise to stay with him.

But it was a promise she couldn't make. Even if she'd gotten used to these countries of time, she was still an existence without a fixed place. She was an Outsider, and always would be.

But it was *because* of her ambiguous existence

that she'd come to Wonderland in the first place.

"Don't go to any other territories in this country," he rumbled. "Don't go to any other *countries*. Not anymore."

She swallowed. If she hadn't moved, then she would never have met Blood of the Country of Diamonds. But now…she didn't want to move again.

Alice nodded her head.

"I'll stay by your side, Blood." Without thinking, her right hand drew up to lie on the left side of his chest. She felt those familiar, gentle reverberations of his ticking clock against her palm. His ticking and her heart shouldn't have overlapped, but her heart gave a pound at the touch against her skin.

But for a moment…she heard a very different sound within herself. She almost thought she heard a hard ticking in her own chest.

Just like the clock ticking in his.

Alice tilted her head in surprise, but before she could make certain, he stole another kiss.

"Mm. Ah…!"

Alice's insides melted into sighs and heat, and she lost the ability to think.

Right then, for that moment only, Alice allowed herself to be completely ruled by Blood. She wasn't going anywhere. She felt it, and with that came relief.

"Blood…"

"You'll stay with me," he breathed into her mouth. "Right?"

He wanted confirmation, a commitment. Alice pulled her lips free and nodded.

"Yeah. I'm staying."

*I'll be here with **you,** the man before me now. No one else.*

She lived in a world where everything constantly changed. Maybe it was foolish to count on anything for sure.

But even so, as she exchanged vows with him, she hoped that her heart would get its payout.

~Epilogue~
Art by Nana Fumitsuki

THANK YOU SO MUCH FOR ALWAYS BEING MY TOUR GUIDE, JERICHO.

DON'T WORRY ABOUT IT.

IT'S MY JOB TO SEE MY GUESTS THROUGH THE BUILDING.

CHATTER

CHATTER

?

CHATTER

CHATTER

CROWD

CROWD

CROWD

BLOOD ?!

ISN'T THIS ENEMY TERRITORY? WHAT'S HE DOING HERE?!

CROWD

313

HEY! IF YOU FEEL LIKE MAKING TROUBLE, DO IT SOMEWHERE ELSE.

RELAX, GRAVE-KEEPER.

I'M JUST HERE TO RETRIEVE MY GIRL-FRIEND-- SHE LEFT MY TERRITORY AND DIDN'T COME BACK.

DON'T MAKE A MESS IN MY MUSEUM.

THAT'S IT?

THAT'S WORTH SCARING AWAY ALL MY GUESTS?

DESERTED

YEAH! SISTER'S BEEN GONE A LONG TIME...

SO BLOOD GOT WOR-RIED--

WHACK

ELLIOT...

KRGH!

314

OF COURSE CUSTOMERS AVOID THE PLACE.

WELL, THE LEADER OF THIS TERRITORY IS A DEAD DODO WALKING.

LISTEN, YOU...

I CAN NEVER TELL IF THESE TWO ARE ACTUALLY COOPERATING...

OR WANT TO KILL EACH OTHER.

....

TAK TAK

TH-THANKS FOR COMING TO GET ME, BLOOD!

I WAS JUST ON MY WAY BACK.

?

BLOOD?

....

315

IT WAS A PRESENT FROM YOUR BOY-FRIEND.

TAKE IT WITH YOU AND NEVER LOSE IT.

PLACE

DON'T BE COLD, YOUNG LADY.

YOU FORGOT THIS.

. . . .

BUT IF I WALK AROUND WITH THIS GIANT THING ON MY HEAD...

EVERYONE WILL KNOW WHO I AM! I'LL BE A WALKING TARGET!

HEH.

FINE-- THEN JUST GO EVERY- WHERE I GO.

THAT MEANS YOU'LL NEVER GET CLOSE TO OTHER MEN. IN ANY CAPACITY.

SST

?

FSSH

!

Priority Ticket
Art Museum

317

UGH, JERICHO SAW THAT! I'M SO EMBARRASSED!

IT'S OKAY. I'LL WELCOME YOU BACK, NO MATTER WHAT YOU WEAR.

PLEASE COME AGAIN.

YOU REALLY ARE A HANDFUL.

ME?

YES, YOU. YOU'RE MAKING YOUR NEXT DATE TO CHEAT ON ME WHILE I'M STANDING RIGHT HERE.

AHEM!

AH!

OH? YOU HAVE SOME EXCUSE?

PLEASE. I'M NOT CHEATING.

DON'T YOU EVER LEARN, WOMAN?

KISS

THEN I'LL HEAR YOU OUT. TAKE YOUR TIME.

GRAB

EEK!

YOU'RE THE ONE WHO SAID I SHOULD INVESTIGATE YOU, ALICE.

319

END

AFTERWORD

I want to take this opportunity to thank you for picking up this book. My name is Sana Shirakawa.

This book is a novelization of QuinRose's *Alice in the Country of Diamonds*. The game is something of a "turning point" in the *Alice* series. There are a lot of mysteries in Wonderland, and this story brings us much closer to the answers.

This particular book centers on Alice and Blood's relationship. And because of that, if you haven't played the game, you might not understand the reason why Blood gives Alice a "certain something." I hope the book leads you to playing the game.

Again, I'd like to thank the many people who helped me so much in the writing of this book.

Editor K. from Ichijinsha Publishing, Nana Fumitsuki, and of course, QuinRose. I'd like to thank them for their patience--they put up with me pestering them for the details on the drastic setting change from the previous games. I also look forward to their support in the future. Thank you!

And finally, to everyone who has been kind enough read this far—thank you so much!